KILLING
FOR SPORT

KILLING FOR SPORT

Inside the Minds of Serial Killers

PAT BROWN

NEW MILLENNIUM PRESS
Beverly Hills

ISBN: 1-893224-93-7

Library of Congress Cataloging-in-Publication Data Available

Text Design: Kerry DeAngelis, KL Design

New Millennium Press
301 North Canon Drive
Suite 214
Beverly Hills, CA 90210

10 9 8 7 6 5 4 3 2 1

DEDICATION

This work is dedicated to all those who stand in support of truth and justice, no matter the cost: the families of homicide victims who will never let the death of their loved one go unanswered, the police investigators who go the extra mile to get a dangerous offender off the street, and all the friends and family who support those fighting for this cause, in spite of the sacrifices and difficulties such work brings to all involved.

TABLE OF CONTENTS

WHY I WROTE THIS BOOK — WHY YOU NEED TO READ IT

Someone needed to tell it like it is.

I have wanted someone to write this book for years. As the CEO of The Sexual Homicide Exchange (SHE), a nonprofit criminal profiling agency handling cold case homicides, I have spent years trying to correct the misperceptions about serial killers that plague families of victims, police investigators, and the general public. I had thought by now some other profiler would have written a book that would provide tools for everyone to use to increase safety and catch killers. Unfortunately, the books that line the shelves of bookstores and libraries instead contain gruesome tales of "real serial killers," tell of FBI men and their "daring captures," or are full of academic analysis obscurely trying to explain the serial killer phenomenon. Not a single book has appeared with facts set forth in a way that everyone can understand and put to use in their life or work.

Why not? The most likely reason is that scary books sell, and "fancy" academic jargon allows the professionals in the field to appear to have some special understanding that only they can comprehend after years of training. While years of experience certainly do lead to increased knowledge and abilities, an awful lot of the solid, useful information can be understood by anyone, if someone would just put it to them plainly. Since no one else has, I will.

The ideas that people form about serial killers are based heavily on what they read in sensational "true crime" books or see on television and in movies. Unfortunately, these depictions are often distorted, leaving us with wrong impressions of how predators choose their prey, commit their crimes, and live their lives. Lacking the proper understanding of serial killers and how they operate, many people walk right into the predator's hands and become another statistic.

Even police investigators, psychologists and profilers fall prey to misconceptions about serial killers and their behaviors; and this lack of accurate knowledge has caused many a homicide case to remain unsolved and allowed many a killer to go on his merry criminal way.

It is my goal with this book to answer your questions with no fluff, no psychobabble, and no ego trips. I went out of my way to be brutally honest, and I think I may have managed to offend just about everyone.

Oh, well.

I *want* you offended—this book is written as much as possible from the point of view of the predator. You need to be offended by his thoughts. More importantly, you, Average

Citizen, need to be able to spot those thoughts as they are forming in the mind of your creepy next-door neighbor. Or, if you are someone working a sexual homicide case, you need to be able to nail the killer sitting cheerfully opposite you in an interview room.

Explaining the motive of a killer in complex psychological jargon may be impressive to other scholars but it does not show us what is in the perpetrator's mind. Offenders do not say, "Today I intend to commit a rape which includes the sexual penetration with my penis into the vaginal cavity of a female in order to placate the anger within me from my troubled youth." More likely he's thinking, "I am going to teach that bitch a lesson." *Teaching that bitch a lesson* has not yet been deemed an official psychological motivator. It does, however, give you, the reader, a realistic look into the thoughts of the criminal who is about to brutally attack you or some innocent teenager on the way home from school. This is the part of the criminal's mind you need to understand. Leave the deep and "meaningful psychology" to the shrinks in hospitals who have lots of spare time to kill with predators who are delightfully medicated into oblivion. You need to be able to save your own butt on the street or put a creep in prison where he belongs.

The goal of this book is to teach **everyone** how to identify predators so we can make our streets safer for all of us.

ONE LITTLE, TWO LITTLE, THREE LITTLE SERIAL KILLERS

Serial killer basics

WHAT IS A SERIAL KILLER?

Brace yourself; I am going to upset a lot of traditionalists.

Going by the "rules," a serial killer is an individual who kills on at least three occasions, with a break between killings to "emotionally cool off" (SHE translation—he takes time after the kills to go back to his "normal life"). Three kills gives our boy a chance to commit his first crime perhaps by accident, the second time for curiosity's sake to see if he *really* liked what happened the first time, and the third time is

> **" *Big deal, death comes with the territory...see you in Disneyland.* "**
> —*RICHARD RAMIREZ*

the proof that he's into the groove and a regular killing machine. (By the way, spree killers and mass murderers are guys who kill on just one occasion in their lives and take out a bunch of people in one big hurrah. These guys usually end up dead at the end of the day.)

Some daring experts have dropped the number of kills needed to be a serial killer to just two. They believe that you can eliminate the need for the evidence of a third kill as "proof" if the first two kills are really nasty. They reason that two brutal rape/murders with a tire iron and duct tape in close proximity to each other is proof enough that you have a serial killer on your hands.

So, here's the million-body question: *Why does it take as many as two?*

It's been a long hard day at school, and Junior plops down on the sofa. He's been looking forward to this all day, crashing out on the couch with a bad TV show. He's got his bag of chips and he's set. He just gets one pitiful bit of fried potato to his lips before mom comes by and snatches the bag away from him and tells him, "Not so close to dinner!" Can we assume that Junior only had the intention of eating that solitary chip?

After years of mustering the courage, the predator makes his first kill. He's been dreaming about this as long as he can remember, fantasizing about what it would be like to administer the lethal measure to another human being, how it would feel to hear the last bits of air leave *his* victim's lungs. He's found his target, and he's set. As he finishes his masterpiece, something goes wrong, and here come the police to arrest him; he's convicted and locked away. Can we assume that this predator only had the intention of killing this solitary victim?

Not on your life.

A serial killer may be better defined as an individual who has decided to avenge himself against society by grabbing his moment of power in a way that excites him most: homicide. He has killed a thousand times in his head by the time he actually places his hands on a real victim. To him, the murder he commits is just a reenactment of his fantasized behavior; and it's a whole lot of fun. He's getting to act out his dirtiest thoughts. If *you* were he, wouldn't *you* want to do it again?

So why not start off totally redefining what a serial killer "is"?

A young man in rural Minnesota was convicted of murder in the third degree. Shawn Padden murdered 18-year-old Greggory Meissner in his own bedroom by whacking Gregg on the back of the head with a bowling pin and then hanging him on the closet door by a hemp rope he had brought to the scene. Convicted in 1998 for a "dangerous act with no intent to kill," Shawn Padden may be out in less than fifteen years because this is his *only* known kill.

Now, going by the two-to-three body rule, we shouldn't pay too much attention to the pictures of decomposing dead boys Padden carried around in his wallet, his history of fire setting, or the small fact that he obsessed over hanging and openly fantasized and talked about how seeing someone hang in real life would be "so cool." It's really not relevant to this man's career as a potential serial killer.

Right?

So we have guys who kill just one person, but might be serial killers. What about when a guy we think is a serial killer goes on a spree and kills a bunch all at once?

Ted Bundy (c'mon, *everyone* knows him, you don't need the bio!) went into a bizarre "hyper killer" mode at the end of his "career" and crashed a couple of sorority houses. Breaking in and killing two young women and brutalizing three others, Bundy broke the "serial killer rules" by escalating to a spree killer. This occasionally happens. Bundy knew law enforcement was closing in to take away his bag of chips, and he was trying to stuff in as many as he could before they showed up.

Oh, wait, are terrorists serial killers?

No, not in the traditional sense, but some of the same type of thinking is at play in the terrorist's mind as in the serial killer's mind. No one grows up happy and well-adjusted and then suddenly decides to become a suicide bomber. As this individual grows up, something in his life causes him to become more and more alienated from his family and mainstream society. Eventually, he seeks out some purpose, some concept, or some ideal that will make his life meaningful and some special action that will make him a very important person, if only for a moment in history. The terrorist is pretty much a kind of mass murderer/serial killer that tacks on a political "reason" for killing innocent people. In his opinion, the people "deserve" to be killed because they represent an enemy of his mission and besides, even if they are innocent, there is always "collateral damage" in war. Fringe political groups and violent terrorist cells are always searching for these kinds of desperate people and when they find them, they can easily "manipulate" them into "killing for the cause." In certain parts of the world, being a terrorist is much "cooler" than being a serial killer.

HOW MANY SERIAL KILLERS ARE THERE OUT THERE?

A whole lot more than the FBI and police are telling us! Law enforcement tends to minimize the presence of serial killers in our communities, so they don't scare the public and so the media doesn't hound them.

However, in the interest of public safety, we must be aware that there may be dangerous offenders living in our neighborhoods.

But I haven't read about any serial killers in my city. Why not?

The young lady found in a dumpster might have a day of front-page coverage, but after that, her family will find their daughter's homicide relegated to the back pages of the paper (if that) where she is quickly forgotten. Let's face it, murder

> *"We serial killers are your sons, we are your husbands, we are everywhere. And there will be more of your children dead tomorrow."*
>
> —*TED BUNDY*

is not good news, and it's just not good publicity for the community if people think they could get killed in their own town!

Since serial killers don't kill nearly as often as Hollywood would have us believe, and sometimes they wait years between kills, attention on their activities fades quickly. Rarely do we read about a half dozen women found dead within a short period of time, à la "celebrity" killer Jack the Ripper. More often, in one locality, you will find four or five run-of-the-mill serial killers who slowly bump off victims over decades.

Let's say a serial killer kills one woman in June of 1994 and another woman in the next county in February of 1997. He hasn't killed in the six years since then; he's going about life as usual, getting up to go to work every day. His life is somewhat stable. Then his wife decides to divorce him or he gets fired from his job. Suddenly we have a new homicide, and the likelihood of this third homicide being seen as related to his previous two is next to nil.

People also seem to forget that serial killers are capable of packing up and moving from their houses and apartments, or even taking drives to other jurisdictions. The serial killers in your town may have just moved in, or may only be there for a brief period of time on business. Serial killers have lives, jobs, and (occasionally) families, and move around just like the rest of us.

When we fail to see the connections between serial homicides and instead label them one-off crimes (SHE Definition—just one-time killings by a mad boyfriend or dealer in a drug deal gone bad), the serial killer knows he can still operate freely. Often the only time connected sexual homicides are labeled the work of a serial killer is when the bodies are dumped in one location, when they occur within a tight period of time, or if there is some extremely obvious element that connects the crimes. At present, a high percentage of the crimes committed by serial killers go unnoted and unsolved, and the number of serial killers tends to be underestimated.

ARE ALL SERIAL KILLERS WHITE?

No, but we're sure that this stereotype makes the non-Caucasian serial killers laugh. Wayne Williams, Timothy Spencer, Charles Ng, Angel Resendez, George Russell and serial snipers John Muhammad and Lee Malvo are just a few of the minority serial killers who have been caught in the United States.

> *Look down on me; you will see a fool. Look up at me; you will see your Lord. Look straight at me, you will see yourself.*
> —CHARLES MANSON

Serial killing is not a product of some weird racial gene in Caucasians that causes serial homicide behavior. Serial killers exist wherever they can get away with their crimes.

So why haven't I heard about serial killers of other races?

There are a number of reasons serial killers of African, Asian, and Hispanic origins are ignored. When the media does report on a serial crime, they tend to focus on stories where the victim is the "All-American" girl. The wealthier, prettier, and whiter she is, the more press she gets. Homicides of minority women often get passed over.

Contributing to this lack of coverage is the greater number of Blacks, Hispanics, and Asians living in urban communities where crime rates are higher. In this setting, serial homicides, as well as other crimes, are under-investigated. Linkage between serial homicides is rare due in large part to overworked police departments and lack of communication between jurisdictions. This reduces the fear of apprehension and makes for a great killing ground for serial killers. Minority serial killers in the United States more than likely exist at the same ratios as white serial killers for the population. Go to Zaire in Central Africa, and you will hear the question, "Are there any *white* serial killers?"

Then why do profiles always read "Male, WHITE..."?

Most likely this myth simply became "truth" after it was stated so many times by the experts. Because crimes against white victims are investigated more thoroughly and more white killers caught, it seemed to the experts that they had proven this concept to be true.

ARE THERE SERIAL KILLERS IN OTHER COUNTRIES?

Absolutely! In any population in the world, you will find serial killers. Some countries have famous serial killers such as England, Russia, South Africa, and Germany. Other countries have horrific serial killings that have never been talked about or made it into print outside of their own regions. Juarez, Mexico is one such area which has suffered from the murder of hundreds of young women in the last decade—young women coming from the rural areas of Mexico to earn money for their families by working in one of the many *maquilladoras* (factories) that have sprung up along the border of Mexico with the United States. We haven't heard all that much up north about the sad situation there or many other areas in the world because little shows up in our newspapers. However, the United States does have a very active media that focuses on sensational local stories, so Americans come off looking like a pretty bad lot!

> **I don't lose sleep over what I have done or have nightmares about it.**
>
> —DENNIS NILSEN

However, it is also true that some countries have cultures that prevent wannabe serial killers from having the opportunity to act out their desires, while other countries have such strict criminal justice systems that serial killers never get a second chance to offend.

ARE THERE ANY WOMEN SERIAL KILLERS?

When most people think of serial killers, they think of rape. They think that serial homicide is a sexual homicide each and every time. However, serial homicide is a crime of power and control, and sex is just *one* way of achieving that.

> " *All I want to do is go back to the prison, wait for the chair and get the hell off this planet, that is full of evil.* "
>
> —AILEEN WOURNOS

Female killers tend to come in more subtle flavors, and compared to their male counterparts, they are far more manipulative—often using methods that are less violent but just as lethal.

Women serial killers tend to pick targets that are closer to home, and their victims are rarely total strangers. With the exception of being part of a serial killer team (where they kill as a couple for their sexual kicks), women tend to kill their husbands, their children, and the kids and patients they care for in their employment.

The normal nurturing role of Mother can generate feelings of tremendous accomplishment for women who love and care for their children. Other women really don't like the kid much to begin with and get little reward from their poor mothering efforts; some of these women also see themselves in competition with their children for attention.

Munchausen's Syndrome by Proxy (MSP) is a nasty little psychological development occasionally found in this group of moms. These women discover that they can receive attention for being "a good and loyal mom" by taking their child to be treated by a doctor. Realizing this is not only a good way to get attention, but also a way to punish the little crumb-snatcher for stealing the attention she wants for herself, she begins to inflict injuries that will manifest as baffling horrible diseases and the serial abuse begins. As the illnesses get progressively worse, the attention she wants increases, and when the child eventually dies (is murdered), there is yet more attention heaped upon the mother that she will be able to manipulate for months to come. Eventually the concern and care begin to dwindle, leaving her to seek attention in the best way she knows how: she must get pregnant and start the process all over again. Mary Beth Tinnings managed to get pregnant and murder *nine* children (including one adopted one!) before the authorities finally got the idea that the deaths of the children weren't natural tragedies.

Day care children and patient killings are another category many women fall into for serial killings. In these cases, the women often appear to do a good job and have fine nurturing skills. Apparently, this is not enough reward. These women need to get their kicks from a heroic lifesaving attempt. They have a bottomless need for attention and must go for the ultimate thrill to achieve their feelings of power and success.

"Angels of Death" are those nurses and physicians who kill their patients. Typically, they select patients whose deaths are not likely to be questioned. Often they administer a lethal dose of medication and wait for the EKG to sound the alarm, and then join in the rush to revive the patient as the Code Blue team arrives. The number of victims these killers are able to accrue is astounding. Because of their careful selection of victims, the fact that fifty patients have died (with their help) on their shift may not come to light for a long, long time.

Childcare "Angels" take a slightly different route to killing. They will simply smother a sleeping infant and then "find" the child in distress, call 911, begin CPR and wait to be the hero. Because infants do not usually show the same physical manifestations of suffocation as adults, spotting a smothering death is difficult for the medical examiner. It usually takes several victims for authorities to "get wise."

Don't women ever commit more violent types of serial homicides?

Sure they do, just not quite as often. Women who marry and murder their husbands are often referred to as "Black Widows." Although many believe they kill purely for financial gain, the underlying motive is still the ability to gain power and control over an individual and society. Sometimes these women advertise in personal ads to get their victims who eventually end up poisoned to death or with a bullet in the back of their head in a "botched robbery."

She ends up the grieving wife and generally picks up and leaves town within a few months of being "widowed."

Some women can be just as vicious in their desires as a male serial killer, just not as "motivated" to act alone, so they team up to get their jollies through helping their boyfriends abduct, torture and kill female victims. They have similar interests, and she's able to meet her needs as well as his. She can use him as an "excuse" for her behavior and still get in on the thrill of killing. More on serial killing teams later.

Lastly, there are a few women that commit straight-up violent serial homicides all by themselves. Prostitute-turned-serial killer Aileen Wournos is one of the rare birds that chose to blow away her male victims without any pretense of love or devotion. She hated them, she killed them, and she was damn proud of it.

WHAT STATE HAS THE MOST SERIAL KILLERS?

> " *I was only following God's orders.* "
>
> —JOSEPH KALLINGER

It sure *seems* like Oregon and Washington State have an awful problem with serial killers. However, when one spends time investigating serial homicides in other states, it is amazing how many there are just about everywhere.

The theories as to why those northwest states have such a serious problem with serial killers range from the weather, to a whole bunch of trees to hide the bodies among, to the theory that weird people move west and simply have no states left before they fall into ocean.

There is really no good research on the topic, so I will refrain from pretending any statistical knowledge. It may well be that just as many serial homicides occur in Florida, but the bodies are dinner for alligators and we are therefore simply unaware of the numbers.

You can still rest assured that your nearest major city probably has at least a handful of bored pathetic souls with nothing better to do than to kill humans for sport.

ARE THERE HOMOSEXUAL KILLERS?

A basic rule of thumb is if the victim of a sexual homicide is male (and not just a witness killed during the murder of a female), chances are very high that the perpetrator is a homosexual or bisexual serial killer. Male victims of these killers can come from both the homosexual and

> " *I really screwed up this time.* "
>
> —JEFFREY DAHMER

heterosexual communities. The only importance of the *victim* being gay or not is in determining where he might have met his killer.

When it comes to the homosexual or bisexual serial killer, Jeffrey Dahmer and John Wayne Gacy are probably the most notable. Each man had his own method of victim selection. Dahmer's victims were gay men he encountered in social situations and brought back to his home. Most of Gacy's victims were heterosexual teenage boys that he would either hire to work for his contracting business or lure into his car for a "joint." Dahmer was more open about his sexuality than Gacy, frequenting gay bars and bathhouses. Gacy, on the other hand, tried continually to lead a "normal" straight life, marrying twice and playing the doting stepfather to his last wife's daughters.

ARE THERE SERIAL KILLER TEAMS?

Of all the things about serial killers, this is one of the most frightening thoughts—that more than one person could be participating in the murders of several individuals for the thrill.

Killing teams tend to be far more brutal than solitary offenders and the amount of time the killers take to torture and kill their victims is much longer. Feeding off of each other's energy and excitement, they work as a tag-team egging each other on.

Teams *usually* have a leader and are male/male or male/female; there are a few historical female/female killing teams, but they seem to be far fewer in number.

> *"She was a hooker. Angelo went and picked her up. I was waiting in the street. He drove around to where I was. I got in the car. We got on the freeway. I fucked and killed her. We dumped the body off and that was it. Nothing to it."*
> —KENNETH BIANCHI

When it comes to male/female teams, the female participants of these deadly duos seem to enjoy the brutality as much as their "leaders"—contrary to the preconceived notions many experts and society in general have about women's roles in such crimes. Granted, it is often difficult to discern how involved in these homicides the women are. Females tend to be able to manipulate the system quite effectively, and they have their male counterparts to blame for "forcing" them to help. In a society very aware of domestic abuse, this ploy often gets the female killer off with a very light sentence.

The all-male teams turn killing into a sport. Some teams literally keep score for age of victim, degree of torture, victim response and duration of kill. Serial killers Roy Norris and Lawrence Bittaker set up a game in which they would abduct, rape and kill girls starting at age thirteen, with the plan of taking a victim of each age (in order) up to age twenty. Using a highly mobile means, they cruised the highways in their van dubbed the "Murder Mack" attempting to fulfill their plans. Their lack of patience meant that they never quite achieved their ultimate goal, but in the process it is believed that they were responsible for the deaths of at least nineteen missing young women.

ARE ALL SERIAL KILLERS BETWEEN THE AGES OF TWENTY AND THIRTY-FIVE?

No, but a whole lot of profilers tend to use those ages. The major reason for this is that males in that age range commit most of the violent crimes. Before age twenty, most young men do not have access to vehicles and have not gotten to the point of finally crossing the killing line; after age thirty-five, incarceration, illness, and death reduce the number of active serial killers in the upper age ranges.

If a profiler is trying to make sure he gets the age question right, it won't hurt if he makes the age range wide enough to encompass a large population of potential suspects; thus the birth of the "age twenty to age thirty-five" cliché.

> " You'll never get me. I'll kill again. Then you'll have another long trial. And then I'll do it again. "
> —HENRY BRISBON

ARE THERE MORE SERIAL KILLERS OUT THERE THAN EVER BEFORE?

Yeah, and there are more people too. Seriously, as the population grows so will the number of serial killers.

> *There are other 'Sons' out there—God help the world.*
> —DAVID BERKOWITZ

The more crowded areas are, the easier it is for killers to get lost in the population. Imagine that you live in a town of five hundred people. You have known these people intimately since the day you were born, so you would find it relatively easy to say, "It's probably 'Weird Bob' who lives on the corner of Ninth and Elm," should an atrocious crime ever occur.

But in a city of a million or more people, good luck.

When a victim is abducted or the body is dumped, there would be a limited number of people in a small town who could have been in the area at the time, while in a large city with skyscrapers, vacant buildings and loads of dumpsters there might be hundreds of folks within a few thousand feet, even if it is straight up.

The more people there are, the more cases there are, and the more overburdened and confused law enforcement may become. Serial killers know the odds are low that they will even be considered a suspect in heavily populated areas and can kill at their leisure without fear of being apprehended.

Today's media also makes us more aware of serial killers. Back in the old days, serial killers didn't get much press. Now serial homicide makes for great copy, and more books (like this one) come out every day to keep us duly informed of the serial killers in our midst.

CREATURE FROM THE BLACK LAGOON

What makes a serial killer

ARE SERIAL KILLERS BORN OR MADE?

This is an argument that will probably never be settled. Nature vs. Nurture...Can a child be born a serial killer? Or is the child a product of his environment? Is it a combination of both?

> " *I'm a sick person. I know that. How could a normal guy do what I did? It was like another guy was inside me.* "
> —ALBERT DE SALVO

Some people believe that the acts of serial killers are so vile that no cultural influences could account for the development of such heinous behavior; therefore, there must be some evil gene or abnormality in their brains that causes them to kill. Others believe that no human being can be doomed from the start with no hope of avoiding such a fate, so it must be cultural. A third group thinks that it is probably a combination of the two.

Once again, I actually believe a fourth point of view might be the most accurate.

To date, there is nothing that has been established in research that supports the presence of an "evil gene" or some bizarre brain abnormality. So where does this abhorrent behavior come from? It would seem that this anti-social behavior must then be learned, but it is not always the sole-contributing factor to the serial killer's behavior. It seems common sense that if you take a child and raise him in a violent household, chances are he or she is going to have a few "issues" with their emotional and psychological development; however, the abuse suffered is not always blindingly obvious.

Our *personalities* begin to develop very early in life, within the first few months. These are not necessarily genetically based, nor are they environmentally based; but they are deeply rooted in who we are from birth. Some children have what might be deemed a pleasant personality, while others have a demanding one. Neither is fundamentally "bad," and each kind of personality can benefit society, as we need all kinds of people to make society work.

The deadliest combination seems to lie in those children who have difficult and demanding personalities and whose lives are then compounded by abuse, neglect, or a subtler dysfunction. The emerging behaviors are then ignored until they escalate to become a violent and psychopathic personality. Consider this family:

A young stepmother was discussing the behaviors of her stepson. She was concerned because the 7-year-old had been expelled from school for a series of bad behaviors. He was overly demanding of attention and time from his teacher (and at home), he had been fondling girls on the playground, had lit a fire in a school trash bin and stabbed a fellow-classmate with a pencil. "Should I be concerned?" she queried (SHE Answer—Hell yes!). As she discussed the issue with the school "counselor," she made excuses for him, and together they minimized the behaviors as a "stage" he was going through and settled on an ADD diagnosis and some meds.

Is this child going to become the next Zodiac killer? I can't make that call. But even very young children can begin displaying anti-social behaviors that should cause concern. It is critical in these early years to intervene with more than a pill and a shrug.

Does this mean that all serial killers come from abusive homes?

Well, according to FBI research, one hundred percent of serial killers have suffered some sort of "child abuse." That sounds pretty damning at first read, and if you go no further than that statistic, it seems like a pretty hefty factor in the making of these killers. But reading about what is defined as "abuse" makes you realize that, heck, you and Wally and Beaver Cleaver were abused too!

The brush used to paint the definition of "childhood abuse" is far too wide. Granted, some serial killers suffer horrendous abuse as children, but there are some serial killers who come from nonviolent homes. On the other hand, I have yet to find a serial killer who has come from a totally functional and strong family; something is always a bit amiss. Are the happenings in these families amiss to the point of real abuse? Not always.

> " *The victim is the dirty platter after the feast and the washing-up is a clinically ordinary task...Occasionally I hear a piece of music which was playing at the time of the killings—then I become extremely disturbed.* "
>
> —DENNIS NILSEN

ARE ALL SERIAL KILLERS GENIUSES?

Hollywood and fiction writers would sure like to make us think so! But keep in mind, a clever story sells and therefore the evil genius serial killer is much more of a moneymaker than the idiot serial killer.

The personality of a serial killer lacks imagination and patience—two requirements for genius work. Rather than displaying "cunning" methods of capture and killing, serial killers tend to borrow ideas and repeat them for lack of creative ability. It is not that serial killers are stupid; they just haven't spent the time and energy on becoming all that brilliant.

Take, for example, the most "clever" serial killer of them all, Ted Bundy. This failed law student drove a gold Volkswagen (gold!) in broad daylight up to a crowded lake where he approached many young ladies with the cunning pick-up line, "My name is Ted." Consequently, the police issued a request to the public for information on a guy named Ted who drives a gold Volkswagen. Ted's girlfriend thought, "Hey! That sounds like *my* boyfriend," and called the police. Unfortunately, the police ignored her information, as well as a couple other folks who called in to rat Ted out. Mr. Bundy eventually got caught, *not* because of brilliant police work, but because of a traffic violation. When Bundy was stopped for speeding, he proceeded to tell the officer he was seeing a movie that wasn't playing, then allowed the officer to search his trunk and find his rape kit consisting of a crowbar, ski mask, rope, handcuffs, wire, and an ice pick! Now ask yourself, "Is this genius?"

The *really* clever acts of many serial killers include hiding in bushes and hitting women over the back of the head when they go by (SHE Definition—Bop and Drop). Others simply break into a house or go to a bar; and really, how terribly clever is it to ask for directions and pull out a gun?

Only a small segment of serial killers work a little harder at planning their crimes in depth and these tend to be the genuine sexual sadists. Because sadism requires the victim to hang around long enough to amuse the offender while he tortures her, he must at least plan a good location and bring a nice set of implements along (or build a cell in the basement and call out for pizza). Even these crimes actually are a bit of a snore if you realize that many of the killers just borrow the ideas from porn sites and books.

Much of the time serial killers are made out to be more intelligent than they are to cover up poor investigative methods. Think about it—if you were a frustrated detective or profiler, wouldn't *you* prefer to say your adversary is a criminal genius, not that you are having trouble catching a dimwit? It makes better press and is far more ego-enhancing if we can catch the criminal mastermind at his game rather than admit, "Uh, yeah, we already interviewed him, but we thought he was just a loser and let him walk. Sure glad that traffic cop stopped him with that severed head in his trunk!"

Are there any good movies out there that show what a serial killer is really like?

Not too many. Most thrillers about these people are pretty silly when they are looked at realistically, but again, I have to admit that fictional killers are created to make money, not to be an accurate portrayal. There are, however, exceptions (which usually bomb at the box office). *An Eye for an Eye* with Sally Field is an excellent film for showing just how much of a creepy loser a serial killer can be. Keifer Sutherland's portrayal of a predator in this film is right on the money—yes, I know the critics hated this film, but if you want to see what these guys are really like (and don't expect Hannibal Lecter), watch this film. Other good choices would be *The Bad Seed, Citizen X, A Stranger Among Us*, and *To Catch a Killer*. Now, if you can't bring yourself to watch movies that bombed publicly, take the time to watch the deepest of all films on the matter of the criminal mind: Stanley Kubrick's *A Clockwork Orange*. This film brilliantly depicts the serial criminal, from *his* point of view, something that no other film has managed to do before or since.

ARE SERIAL KILLERS EVIL?

Some people believe that good and evil are completely separate entities. *We* tend to think of ourselves as good while *they* are the evil ones. Because serial killers commit such horrible crimes, we believe that they must be completely evil. Yet many of us commit similar crimes on a less violent and more legal basis.

It is not illegal for young men to pick up young ladies in bars. They can take them home, have unprotected sex with them, and be completely unconcerned about

> " *I saw the light over the confessional and the voice said: That's the person to kill.* "
> —HERBERT MULLIN

their emotional well-being and the possibility of infecting them with a disease or causing a child to be born into the world unwanted. Some men even think it is no big deal to lie to get what they want that night. They justify their behavior by telling themselves that an adult female is responsible for the choices she makes and therefore they themselves are not responsible for the consequences.

It's as if there is a long continuum of morality. Some folks are at the really "good" end of the spectrum and finish their lives as saints burning on piles of dried timber. Some end up as monsters who burn others on piles of dried timber. The rest of us are somewhere in between. The actions of people can be judged as "good" or "evil," not necessarily the people themselves. We all have our moments of monster, and our moments of saint.

Serial killers are no exception. It's not so much "this person is evil" as it is that this person has become so self-centered that his acts exclude concern for anyone other than himself (SHE tech talk—Narcissism). Certainly his *acts are evil* when compared with what society has decided is normal and nice, but it does not necessarily mean *he* is evil.

ARE MANY SERIAL KILLERS INTO SATANISM?

Not nearly as many as are into the "traditional" faiths.

A good many serial killers have strong feelings about Christianity and righteous behavior. Often the religious hypocrisy they witnessed growing up has helped turn them against society and made them question what is right and wrong. Even in later years, many serial killers still have a fascination with good and evil and spend much time in churches and in religious discussion. In jail, they often become avid Bible readers, although certainly much of this is just a ploy to sucker parole boards into giving them an early release ("I was evil, but now I'm saved!").

> *" There is no happiness without tears, no life without death. Beware! I am going to make you cry. "*
>
> —LUCIAN STANIAK

Many serial killers misuse religious concepts to excuse their behavior. From seeing themselves as holy avengers during their crimes to condemning their acts afterwards, they seem to struggle to find excuses for what they do in any religious text ("If GOD says it's okay....").

Some serial killers stumble upon Pierce Anthony's *For Love of Evil* (probably because the author's last name begins with "A" and it is at the beginning of the sci-fi section of the school library). A well-written science fiction book, the story focuses on the roles of God and Satan and the need for both of them to balance out the world. Searching for ways to excuse their desires, serial killers extract from books like these only what they need to justify their behavior.

"Relativism" is a philosophical concept that serial killers just *love*. Relativism tries to establish that all moralities are equal; that being a vicious serial killer is just as important as being a charitable saint. Serial killers twist this notion to justify their behavior by saying that "without evil, you wouldn't know good," and brush aside their behaviors as simply part of a great cosmic balancing act.

A number of budding serial killers also become fascinated with *The Satanic Bible* and role-playing games like "Dungeons & Dragons" and "Werewolf: the Apocalypse." Both the book and the games combine power and the concepts of relativism to make for a comfortable way to justify any and all acts of behavior. Role-playing, especially taking the role of "Dungeon Master" or "Storyteller," also helps budding psychopaths to set up alternative universes where *their* rules are enforced. When psychopaths become involved in these activities, the line between reality and game becomes blurred in their minds. They end up superimposing their version of a fantasy game on top of reality (where the rest of society lives) and living by their own rules of play.

Now, just because your son likes to play these types of games, it doesn't mean he's about to run out and hack up the neighborhood. As with any hobby or game, most folks just want to have fun; very few take it to a level of real scariness. You only need to become concerned when your child seems wrapped up in the game to the point where he or she uses it to escape from "real life"—some have been known to go as far as trying to perform magic or complex rituals outlined in the gaming guides. In gaming societies, these folks are called "twitchers" and they find themselves quickly excluded from the normal gaming circle.

Interestingly enough, fascination with vampires is also evident among some serial killers, for reasons few people realize. Vampires *are* serial killers who have justified their biting of victims as necessary for survival. Once again, books and role-playing games have helped romanticize this form of serial violence to a level of acceptability among young people that budding serial killers find very convenient.

ARE SERIAL KILLERS PSYCHOTICS OR PSYCHOPATHS?

Very few serial killers ever exhibit psychotic behavior (SHE definition—behavior that convinces us that the individual had NO clue as to what was right or wrong, normal or abnormal, or if what he is doing at that moment is totally nuts!)

> " *I was a greedy, ravenous individual, hungry for life, determined to rise from the bottom.... it wasn't me!* "
> —JACK UNTERWEGER

Kevin Devon Murphy was charged in June of 2000 with the stabbing death of eight-year-old Kevin Shifflett in Alexandria, Virginia. He stabbed Kevin in broad daylight in the boy's great-grandmother's front yard in front of witnesses, then jumped into a taxi and disappeared. Murphy was arrested in connection with this murder after he set his hotel room on fire with a cigarette left burning on the bed and refused to come out of the shower when firefighters came in to save his life. This guy really was a burrito short of a combination platter.

Murphy *might* have become a serial killer if he had managed to croak off a couple more people and, by pure luck, not get caught. Most psychotic serial killers don't rack up many victims because they take little notice of where they kill, what evidence they leave, or what other bizarre behavior they exhibit that causes people to point and say, "What about *that* weirdo?" when asked if they have any good suspects in a local homicide.

A psychotic is just too easy to catch.

On the other hand, psychopaths give law enforcement migraine headaches. Psychopaths (SHE definition—a personality best described as "egocentric" and "anti-social": "Either you are useful or in the way.") know darn well what they are doing. They know what society thinks is right and wrong, and they don't care. They simply want to do what makes them happy and get away with it.

Psychopathic behaviors like pathological lying, grandiose thinking, and manipulation (among many others) coupled with an obsession with violence may lead to homicide. But the desire of these men to stay free and live their lives as they please makes them cautious enough to not commit their crime at a bus stop during rush hour. These killers take great care to make sure there are no witnesses, and because psychopaths don't walk around noticeably ranting and drooling, the citizenry may not be able to easily match the kill with the killer.

Psychopaths are a bit harder to catch.

DO ALL SERIAL KILLERS HAVE THE HOMICIDAL TRIAD OF BEDWETTING, FIRE SETTING, AND ANIMAL TORTURE?

When they do, it's really cool. It makes 'em a heap easier to identify as serial killers! Unfortunately, most of them don't stay true to the "triad." Recognizing specific troubling behaviors in children and young people is critical, but the triad itself does not show up in every serial killer's past.

> "When I was a boy I never had a friend in the world."
>
> —HEINRICH POMMERENCKE

What does hold true are the issues the triad presents. When children feel they have no control over their environment, behavioral problems tend to crop up. As they struggle to gain some kind of power over their lives and others in it, they often resort to anti-social behaviors. The twelve-year-old girl who takes pleasure in upsetting and then smacking an animal is most certainly one to watch for serious delinquent behaviors in the future. Children who are unable to gain their parents' or peers' attention in positive ways will find other ways to gain power and control.

One certainly should not ignore the FBI findings concerning the homicidal triad if it does show up in a young person, because these behaviors may be the precursor to worse crimes as the child grows up. The "crimes" that make up the triad are easily committed by children with budding anti-social behaviors, and will have to do until the kiddies have the physical strength, maturity, or mobility to commit bigger crimes. Fire-setting and animal torture can be accomplished at home or just down the block. An eight-year-old Mike DeBardeleben would have been hard pressed to arrange an appointment with a realtor at a vacant house as a prospective homebuyer (setting up his ruse to rape and kill); but he sure as heck could set the neighbor's tool shed on fire.

DO SERIAL KILLERS HATE THEIR MOTHERS?

Blame Freud for this wee myth.

The fact is, serial killers are just angry and jealous of those in power. Often the mother of the serial killer is assumed to be the domineering battle-ax who beat poor junior to the point where he just had to kill women. The relationship between killers and their mothers is no different from the relationships we all have with our moms. It's a bit of a love/hate thing. It's just that serial killers have more of an issue with any person in power. Many serial killers actually have more anger at Dad or at having no dad. Mom is often the one who intervenes to protect Junior (sometimes overprotecting Junior) and he depends on Mom to take care of him, even as an adult.

> " *I must slay a woman for revenge purposes. To get back at them for all the suffering they caused me.* "
>
> —DAVID BERKOWITZ
> (AN ENTRY FROM HIS PRISON DIARY)

Ed Kemper is an example of someone who clearly did despise his mom—not so much because she was a woman, but because she definitely abused her power over him. He didn't much like her parents, either, because he shot them when he was a teen. After he got out of the mental hospital, he killed six coeds. Finally, he ended his career with the disposal of Mom and one of her friends.

It's important to understand that serial killers choose women as victims for a number of different reasons, not just because

Mrs. Bates was in the basement yelling at poor Normie. Women are small, there's a heck of a lot of them, and they scream real good when you torture them. (I'll discuss this more seriously later.)

One last bit of proof that the "Victim Represents Bad Mom Theory" is all wet is the interesting fact that homosexual serial killers commit same sex killings. Either these guys don't have the same issues with Mom as the heterosexual killers or someone has just been out to blame Mother for everything.

What about guys who kill women who look like their mother/sister/girlfriend?

On occasion, there is a victim who looks quite similar to one of the killer's female relatives or the first girlfriend who rejected him. While sometimes a serial killer may indeed be attracted to a victim who looks like someone else he would like power over, often the resemblance is more a coincidence of similar racial features abundant in the community where he lives. Other times, our desire to see a match between a victim and someone in the killer's life leads us to note those features that look alike and ignore the ones that don't.

When white serial killers kill black women and black serial killers kill white women, this theory is blown out of the water.

Can watching pornography lead to serial killing?

Now before I answer this question, you have to promise not to go burn down the Playboy mansion.

> *"She was giving me oral sex, and she got carried away... So I choked her."*
> —Arthur Shawcross

As a serial killer progresses towards his actual offense he will seek to justify his thoughts and actions by validating them (SHE definition—have someone else say "I do it too, so no, you're not a pervert!") with people they may deem as peers.

Pornography, itself, is a normal activity on the road to growing up. Reading magazines like *Playboy* and *Penthouse* is a not-abnormal and even healthy part of being a guy; let's face it: naked women are pretty to look at.

The problem we have in today's society is the availability and kind of images young people can access. Once upon a time, your seventeen-year-old boy would be caught with just a couple of girlie magazines under the bed. These women were naked but somewhat humanely posed. In order for this young man to have gotten more graphic pornography, he would have had to try to sneak into the XXX building on the outskirts of town and lay out twenty bucks for one glossy magazine without getting busted for being underage. Today your son need only sit down at his home computer and within seconds, free of charge, he can access thousands of images of women participating in all variations of sex—gang bangs, bestiality, and bondage—and, even worse, he can visit rape, torture and murder sites.

Now, instead of seeing a few pictures of girls exposing their breasts, impressionable boys can see women being abused and humiliated. Worse, they see women as permitting this abuse and liking it. A budding serial killer can form the idea that women are sluts and deserving of being raped, and he can also get lots of ideas on how to do it.

If you find your son perusing plain old pornography (women with bad make-up jobs and sexually explicit positions), there really isn't cause to worry. But if your son is spending more and more time viewing extremely hard-core and violent porn, then you probably should consider that a big yellow flag—a big yellow flag on fire.

ARE SERIAL KILLERS SEXUALLY ABUSED AS CHILDREN?

Some serial killers have suffered horrific sexual abuse, while others attain adulthood untouched and virginal. It is often quite hard to determine the level of sexual abuse in a family because many family members are reluctant to admit such abuse, and many serial killers exaggerate it to gain pity from the jury in the sentencing phase of the trial.

> "*If I gave a shit about the parents I wouldn't have killed the kid.*"
> —CLIFFORD OLSEN

Once again we have to fight the broad generalization that they were all sexually molested in brutal and horrid ways and focus instead on what is fact. Enduring actual sexual abuse as children is exceedingly rare in serial predators, and as I mentioned before, the term "abuse" as it is applied to the personal lives of predators in their pre-offense years is hazy and at best an over-generalization.

It is a common myth that the horrible behaviors of the serial killer stem from horrible abuse as children. Believe it or not, you can actually figure out how to abuse another human being without having been taught by another individual. We decide which behaviors make us feel good, which behaviors make us feel bad, and which ones serve our purposes. We also learn at a very young age that our actions can evoke an emotional response from others, and we learn how to manipulate those feelings to get what we want.

The use of sex in a humiliating and demeaning way does not have to be personally experienced by the budding serial killer. He may develop the use of sex as a means to gain power and control over another individual from all that he has learned from society. You don't need to be abused to understand that one of the most vulnerable times in life is when you're naked in bed. Sex brings with it a number of emotions—it's a personal act, and learning to exploit a vulnerable and emotional moment is fairly easy to figure out. Sadism (SHE definition—Making someone else feel bad makes me feel real good) can come in many forms in "normal" folk as well as serial killers. The misuse of words, sex, and household tools make for a painful and humiliating experience for any sexual partner. In the hands of a serial killer, these abuses are taken to the extreme.

WHY DOES EVERYONE ALWAYS SAY, "HE SEEMED LIKE SUCH A NORMAL GUY"?

There seems to be a bit of a dividing line for the folks who say this. The casual acquaintance or next door neighbor, who only knew the serial killer on a fleeting basis, will report him to be as "normal as the next guy"; friendly and even helpful.

> "*I wanted to help her, I just didn't know how to tell her that I killed her child.*"
>
> —ARTHUR GARY BISHOP

People who have spent any amount of time with these guys (like ex-girlfriends and coworkers) will say, "Yeah, he was creepy!" Rarely will you find people who are long-time close personal friends of these killers (as a rule, they seem to lack in the "buddy" department—although they will tell you otherwise). So if you want an opinion from someone who has known the killer for a long time, you will need to ask the family. Oddly enough, most family members (except Mom) will tell you that he creeps them out too.

Their psychopathic personalities cannot stay hidden on a long-term basis. Hang around long enough and dirty habits like pathological lying, grandiosity (SHE Definition—"I was a Vietnam war hero and was dismissed from the FBI for finding out too much about the President"), verbal abuse of women, and the attitudes of "I'm always right" and "people are always out to get me" start to surface.

It's as if people expect serial killers to babble incoherently and have a nasty hunchback; Mother Nature hasn't done us that favor. You really don't get to see the questionable parts of their personalities until after you've known them awhile. A serial killer actually leads a fairly normal life between kills. He's not living in the sewers and surfacing only to rape and murder. He has to mow the lawn, go to work, eat, keep up appearances, and have enough money for pornography. He's not a twenty-four-hour-a-day murder machine.

A serial killer, while he looks normal enough, is not normal; nor is he just weird in an acceptable way. He is weird in a way that says, "I couldn't care less about you or anything you value." Watch out for this kind of guy. He is a lot more dangerous than the boogeyman we think we should be watching out for.

US AND THEM

There are differences...aren't there?

ARE SERIAL KILLERS ALL POOR, OR ARE THERE RICH SERIAL KILLERS?

Another classic line of the bulk-standard "profile" is that the killer will work in a menial job and be dependent on family for financial support. While this is often

> *"My aim was pretty good."*
> —FRANK G. SPISAK, JR.

true, especially when the killer is in his late teens and early twenties (as is true with many young people), some serial killers keep skilled jobs for years and have their own homes; a few have even been quite wealthy.

Let's start with why many of the serial killers aren't doing so well with employment and finances. The personality problems I noted in the last question make it difficult for these guys to stay in school, not get booted out of the military, and not piss off people on their jobs. Consequently, they often have difficulty getting higher-paying, long-term work. Being good manipulators, they then tend to use female relatives and girlfriends (read: suckers) for places to live, vehicles, and help with the bills. Often killers will go from living situation to living situation as jobs come and go and relationships fail. However, it is important to understand that at some point in the serial killer's life he may appear to be doing very well. Check his history and see if this is just something temporary.

There are some serial killers who buck this trend and manage to do a bit better. It seems this group does a little bit better at acting the role of "normal person." They still tend to work at jobs less skilled than one would think they should be able to handle. Again, this is due to lack of patience, personality conflicts, and also a lack of interest in the actual job itself. Work for the serial killer is mostly a method of staying afloat and solvent so that he can continue his other manipulations and pursue his "hobby."

John Wayne Gacy was a reasonably successful contractor. He ran a small firm and employed a great number of teenage boys (read: victims). He looked pretty darn successful. On closer examination, you'll find an employer who would often refuse to pay salaries and sexually harassed, raped and killed some his employees—things I'm sure the Better Business Bureau would frown upon.

Wealthy killers are fairly rare, but they do exist. If an individual actually had the wherewithal to work hard enough to achieve wealth, it is most likely that he would have been winning enough in the game of life not to find killing other people necessary to feel in control and powerful. This kind of person will have found other ways of using people to get what he wants.

Seeming exceptions to this are the infamous H.H. Holmes and Christopher Wilder. Holmes actually built a bizarre castle by posing as the doctor he failed to become and bilking women and contractors out of their money. He was an all-around criminal, serial killing for fun and using the money he got off his victims to continue his abnormal habits.

Christopher Wilder came to America from Australia and made a bunch of money in the construction business. Because of his careless criminal behavior, he finally got in big trouble and went on a spree, abducting and killing women as he drove across the country. He ended up dead at the end of this spree and thus ended his wealthy lifestyle.

One last type of serial killer who has a bit of money is the doctor who decides to off his patients. It is a rare achievement for a serial killer to make it through medical school due to his inability to adhere to rules. However, this type of serial killer is a bit of a "late bloomer," exhibiting psychopathic tendencies throughout medical school and quietly gaining steam towards serial killing as he finds he is unable to attain the power he thought he would get as a doctor.

DO SERIAL KILLERS ALL LIVE WITH THEIR MOTHERS?

Let's expand on this question from what I said before. Norman Bates was held up as the "typical" serial killer in Hollywood—until Hannibal Lecter came along.

> " *I hate a bitchy chick.* "
> —GERALD STANO

It's not always Mom (although she's an easy target) a serial killer decides to mooch off of; as a matter of fact, most any woman will do. Women have this horrible habit of being softhearted. Women tend to believe a person should get a second chance and that he can be saved with just the right kind of help. Mothers, especially, feel duty bound to "love the unlovable" and care for their scary-as-hell sons.

Serial killers like to target women of strong religious faith, women who are lonely for male companionship, and any woman with a family connection whom they can guilt-trip into helping them. Even if they don't live with these women, often they will use them as avenues to getting jobs, borrow money from them, use their vehicles, and keep them around for alibis and window-dressing.

Serial killers also rent rooms and live with "friends." Short-term arrangements are not uncommon, because no job equals no rent money, and strange behavior makes people ask you to leave as soon as possible.

WHAT KIND OF WORK DO SERIAL KILLERS DO?

What's with all the security guard jobs?! Granted, not all of them work as security guards, but it sure seems like a lot of them do. Serial killers crave power and control but rarely can pass the police psychiatric exam. However, it is darn easy to get unarmed security work with the pressing need in stores and malls for loss prevention personnel. The only requirement to get this job seems to be the lack of a felony record, and rarely is much of a background check conducted. If you breathe, you're hired!

> *The demons were protecting me. I had nothing to fear from the police.*
>
> —DAVID BERKOWITZ

Security work does require a certain amount of personal interaction, and the more gregarious serial killers tend to go for this sort of thing. The more antisocial may work in jobs requiring fewer people skills such as mechanical or janitorial work.

Temporary work is also popular among serial killers. The handyman type of job only requires the guy to show up at the door asking for work (this sometimes results in the employer not needing anything else fixed around the house ever again!). Serial killers prefer jobs where, because of high turnover and low pay, employers will pretty much hire anyone, regardless of criminal record or work history (in the words of one such desperate employer, they hire anyone who is "not total pond scum").

Truckers seem to be in a distinct category. This job does not require much face-to-face social interaction. Some serial killer truckers do okay on the CB, and trucking requires only limited human interaction at loading areas and truck stops; it's the perfect job for the kind of serial killer who loves driving and trolling for victims.

DO SERIAL KILLERS HAVE PRIOR CRIMINAL RECORDS?

This question should probably come with a disclaimer. Just because he doesn't have a record, doesn't mean he hasn't committed other crimes—it just means he hasn't been caught.

A guy doesn't just wake up one day and think "I'm gonna be a serial killer"; there is a natural progression to these crimes. They don't just happen out of the blue. These guys all seem to follow a happy little path of destruction; and their crimes reflect it.

When the killer becomes brave enough to leave the comfort of his own home and pornography, he begins his real-world invasion. Voyeuristic behaviors are usually the first serious red flag in serial behavior, and can vary widely from "Peeping Tom" to "Sneak and Stand" (SHE Definition —those guys that appear out of nowhere and are just standing there, staring at you). From Peeping Tom, we head to frotteurism (SHE Definition—rubbing and touching an item or person for no obvious reason other than being a bloody pervert!) and other forms of personal space invasion. After our boy has reached this level, he will go on to stealing personal items; lifting items of little value from friends, coworkers, and relatives (SHE note—a whole lot of guys seem to like to steal change—most likely because this is something a person has handled and saved for a while—or maybe it's just something they don't think will be missed too much).

He now moves on to new personal and sexual levels: lingerie. He may visit laundry rooms of apartment buildings or actually break and enter into a woman's bedroom and snatch items from her drawers. Sometimes he will add a note to the woman that increases the feeling of invasion, leave panties

> *"You feel the last bit of breath leaving their body. You're looking into their eyes. A person in that situation is God!"*
> —TED BUNDY

strewn on her bed or bubble gum stuck in the crotch of a pair; he may even leave roses—anything to further upset and humiliate the victim. Sometimes, there's a sub-level to these acts of invasion that adds a touch of violence, such as cutting out crotches of the panties. This stronger message shows his contempt for his victim and allows him to feel the beginnings of the actual physical assault.

Women rarely report Peeping Toms or lingerie theft and mutilation to the police. Both the victims and law enforcement tend to minimize these behaviors as creepy but not really dangerous. Stealing someone's knickers is not a felony offense, so there isn't much in the way of punishment that can be handed out.

If Peeping Toms and lingerie abductors were taken seriously, we would have a highly effective first line of defense in stopping serial homicide. Ignoring these petty crimes keeps budding serial killers off suspect lists and well below law enforcement radar until it's too late.

Do serial killers ever just rape before they commit sexual homicide, and do they ever go back to just raping?

Rape is sometimes the first violent interaction between the fantasy life of the budding killer and his victim. During this event, he may accidentally (or not) kill his victim. He may at that point decide raping is his kick and stop at this act of violence, or he may decide that killing is even more entertaining. He may also decide he doesn't want to worry about leaving a live witness to the crime, and since dead folks don't talk, dead is better.

If he has chosen to kill, the now-serial killer may continue to always kill, or he may sometimes "just" rape (or he may kill but not rape). The choices are his, the power is his, and it is quite an ego boost to play God and get to make that choice. Occasionally, a serial killer suspends offing his victims after doing so for a long period. This might be for a number of reasons, not the least of which is to get the police off of his back; but also because killing people is a lot of work when you take into consideration the energy required to get rid of evidence and dispose of the body. He may just need the vacation.

DO SERIAL KILLERS COMMIT OTHER CRIMES WHILE BEING SERIAL KILLERS?

Aside from the obvious crimes that come along with serial killing like kidnapping, rape, and assault, many killers have a history of "crap crimes" (SHE definition—crimes you wonder why they bothered to commit).

> " The sixth commandment— 'Thou Shalt Not Kill' —fascinated me...I always knew that some day I should defy it. "
> —JOHN CHRISTIE

Traffic violations head up this list. Because serial killers think following rules is unnecessary, expired tags on their cars are quite common and can lead to being stopped and caught with rape kits and body parts. Speeding is also quite common, as is not having the car registration, one's license, or driving a car with busted taillights.

Theft can be a part of the serial killer's record. Sometimes the need for rope and knives leads one to exit the hardware store without visiting the register. Not only do you get the item free, you aren't seen buying it either. Other kinds of theft are quite popular among losers who are short on money. Serial killers don't have much respect for other people's property anyway, so it is no particular concern of theirs if your silverware collection ends up in a pawnshop.

Burglary is another form of invasion and is fine practice for rape and homicide. It is important to note here that while sexual homicide may be the most pleasurable form of invasion for our offender, this doesn't mean he can't enjoy the "lesser" forms. These crimes are not as time and energy intensive and still keep the feeling of being in power stimulated. Other crimes may include trespassing (another form of invasion), assault, indecent exposure, weapons charges, and fraud (particularly popular among sexual sadists).

Then you have "criminals in overdrive" (SHE definition— the kind of criminal who commits a great many felonies and does just about every kind of crime, including sexual homicides, for shits and grins), who may have extensive records and go on crime sprees with total abandon.

One should be aware that many criminal records are heavily watered down. For example, after plea-bargaining and reduced charges, a serial killer may only have one indecent exposure charge (a failed sexual assault behind a tree) and one burglary (a completed rape in the victim's home that the prosecutor didn't think he could prove in court) on his record. Some serial killers may have committed a dozen rapes or homicides and have no record at all, because they have never been caught or all charges against them have been dropped.

DO SERIAL KILLERS HAVE WIVES OR GIRLFRIENDS?

De Nile ain't just a river in Egypt.

Amazingly enough, these anti-social creepy weirdos still manage to find women

> *"I don't believe in man, God nor Devil. I hate the whole damned human race, including myself... I preyed upon the weak, the harmless and the unsuspecting. This lesson I was taught by others: Might makes right."*
>
> —CARL PANZRAM

willing to have long-term relationships. Young women tend to be more of the mindset of "I can change him. Deep down he's really a nice guy (if he would just stop hitting me)" and older women seem to minimize and justify bizarre behaviors by saying, "He's had a tough time, and he just needs an understanding woman (besides, I haven't had a date in over a year)." It is not that the woman can't see the peculiar behaviors of her serial killer lover; she just finds the positives outweigh the negatives.

Take for example, the wife of serial killer Mike DeBardeleben, who claimed she had no idea what she was getting into when she married him. However, on one of their early dates he proudly showed her a phony driver's license he had made in his basement. On their next date, he showed her the counterfeit money he had made and bragged about his abilities. Still, this young woman went ahead and married Mr. Master Forger, then wondered why her husband turned out to be a less than ideal citizen and mate.

Sometimes, though, it takes the serial killer years to find such a woman, and he may fit the profile of a loner for a long time. When he finally finds a woman willing to ignore everything about him, she doesn't seem to mind the human breast paperweight on the desk and the frozen feet in the fridge.

DO SERIAL KILLERS HAVE DRUG AND ALCOHOL PROBLEMS?

"The offender has a history of alcohol and drug abuse" is yet another profile cliché that is an over-generalization. More often than not, you will see the same casual use of chemicals by a serial killer as by your average non-killing loser.

> " *I would cook it, and look at the pictures and masturbate.* "
> —JEFFREY DAHMER

It is true that some will use chemicals prior to their attacks or kills. However, contrary to the popular misconception, drugs and alcohol do not create the desire to commit the crime. What they do is reduce the fear of failure (SHE definition—"liquid courage"). Likewise, after the crime, many believe that the killer is freaking out about his bad deed and is drowning his guilt in a bottle of Jack Daniels. But, again, the alcohol isn't imbibed as a way to dull the horror of his act, but as a numbing agent to reduce the fear of capture.

There are some serial killers who won't touch the stuff though! These boy scouts of serial homicide see themselves as clean-cut superheroes. They psych themselves up for their crimes by envisioning themselves as masters of the universe who can't possibly fail to crush their enemies. These are the killers most likely to go get a hamburger after the kill and immerse themselves in church and community activities. Blending back into the woodwork lessens the fear of capture without using anything to change the brain chemistry.

WHAT ARE THE FAVORITE BOOKS OF SERIAL KILLERS?

> *"Yes, I did it, but I'm a sick man and can't be judged by the standards of other men."*
>
> —JUAN CORONA

The Bible, the Koran, or the Satanic Bible is often found on the nightstands of serial killers. They like to quote from these when it is useful, and they also seem to like the good/evil dichotomy involved. It is doubtful they actually read that much of these books, but just find a few good supporting arguments for their perverse way of thinking (most flavors of psychopaths from racists to rapists seem to like to do this).

Serial killers (and assassins) seem to gravitate towards *Catcher in the Rye*, the American coming-of-age story that is better read as a coming-of-psychopath story. The self-centered Holden Caulfield is an irritating whiner who complains that everyone is a phony but himself. Serial killers think, "How true this is, except that kid is a bit of a phony and I'm not." This is the typical "I can do no wrong and it's everyone else's fault" attitude serial killers carry with them 24/7, and this book identifies those feelings from the point of view of the narcissistic Caulfield.

One book in particular, *The Collector*, seems to be an all-around favorite. Written by John Fowles, the book details the kidnapping of a young girl and her relationship with her abductor. The orchestration of his crime and his collection of beautiful things falls neatly into place. Serial killers seem to miss the point that the serial killer protagonist plans to kill his victim from the beginning, even though he elaborately pretends not to and eventually faults the victim for causing her own death. Serial killers don't catch the intended meaning and instead jump right on the bandwagon and think, "Yeah, it was the bitch's fault." Consequently, this is a very good book for serial killers to identify with.

The literature and film choices for serial killers seem pretty odd at first glance. It's not the hacker-slasher movies and books you would expect, but rather a strong interest in self-centered characters, science fiction, comic books, super-heroes, war stories, and knights and medieval times.

Fantasy is a critical part of the serial killer's world. With his crimes, he creates an alternative universe where, like the heroes of the stories he reads, he has power beyond imagination and never loses a battle. The proclivity towards fantasy literature illustrates and enhances this.

DO SERIAL KILLERS HAVE HEROES?

Some serial killers get their ideas to rape, torture and kill from places other than well-known serial killers. Granted, serial killing is not really an avant-garde concept, but they don't all read up on Ed Gein, Ted Bundy and John Wayne Gacy and say "Hey, I wanna do that!"

> *What I did is not such a great harm, with all these surplus women nowadays. Anyway, I had a good time.*
>
> —RUDOLPH PLIEL

While many killers, after incarceration, will say that they can identify with other serial killers and their motives, they rarely say that they were inspired to commit their crimes by those who had "gone before." They have their individual motives that don't usually involve the mentorship of other killers. Killers who find "inspiration" are not usually seeking to replicate the crimes of the "celebrities" but rather "one-up" them in body count or brutality. Often the "hero" is not a celebrity killer, but a person closer to home. Someone they could look up to, who seemed to get what he wanted no matter the means—and if people didn't respect him, they feared him.

If they can't find a hero in real life, they often look to the silver screen for the macho hero or even the anti-hero. Popular with killers is *Predator*, the Arnold Schwarzenegger flick about an army/mercenary fighter in combat with a deadly alien predator. It is hard to know which the killer identifies with—the army man or the alien—but both are vicious killers, so take your pick.

Again, just because your son likes these kinds of books and movies doesn't mean he is a monster in the making…unless he tells you, "Freddy Krueger is my hero because he can make people bleed." In that case you should run—don't walk—to the nearest competent therapist.

BETTER YOU THAN ME

A short course in victimology

DO SERIAL KILLERS ALWAYS CHOOSE VICTIMS OF THE SAME RACE?

"Serial killers prefer to hunt within their own ethnic group…"

Ahem.

I'm afraid I have a few issues with this…

There's an amendment that needs to be made to this bit of serial killer stereotyping. Serial killers prefer to kill in their comfort zones. If he's a white guy who is comfortable in a predominantly Hispanic area, chances are he'll kill Hispanic women. The only reason many serial killers tend to kill within their own race is because there are usually a whole lot of women of their own race around where they live. For those who live in racially mixed neighborhoods or work in an area with other races predominating, his comfort zone may expand, and he may kill across racial lines.

> " *I thought 'God, what have I done?' …I realized I would be in serious trouble. I thought the best way out of the mess was to make sure she could not tell anybody.* "
> —PETER SUTCLIFFE

This is not to say that if a serial killer has a preference for a certain race or look (we're all attracted to certain qualities, killers are no exception), he won't try for that. But, if the ideal girl doesn't show up, he might kill whoever does.

People often assume that all choices the killer makes are based on some ideal he has; reading far more into race than really applies. John Lennon's assassin and wanna-be serial killer, Mark Chapman, was believed to want to emulate the musician to the point that he even married a woman of Asian descent—like Lennon had.

Wow! What a nut!

Until you read a bit further. Chapman had moved to Honolulu, Hawaii, a city where Caucasian people are the minority and the majority of the population is of Asian and Polynesian heritage. It is perfectly reasonable and not at all bizarre that Chapman was comfortable in an Asian population and thus married an Asian woman. It's a matter of comfort, and while it seems natural that we would be most comfortable within our own race, this is not always the case.

DO SERIAL KILLERS PICK VICTIMS THAT LOOK ALIKE?

Most people believe they do, and use Ted Bundy as an example.

Set your Way-Back machines to the 1970's for a moment and think…

Bundy seemed to love young women with dark hair, parted down the middle. Now take out any 1974 high school yearbook and ask yourself, "What's with all the hair parted down the middle?" Had Bundy taken it upon himself to seek young women with hair not parted down the middle, we would have had something interesting. The fact is Bundy fancied college-aged women, and the 1970's was just a bad hair decade.

> *I saw women dancing around the golden calf and I thought they were a fickle lot. I knew I would have to kill.*
>
> —HEINRICH POMMERENCKE

More recently Chandra Levy, a government intern, went missing in Washington D.C. Soon there was speculation that she and two other women were victims of a serial killer. Several journalists took pains to point out how "similar" these women were. In their view, these were obviously connected homicides because all the women were professional, they were all dark-haired and looked alike (okay, so they all had different ethnic backgrounds and only people from Sweden would think they looked alike), and, most importantly, they pointed out, they were all from California.

Imagine this scene:

> *Mr. Serial Killer (half-asleep from spending six hours looking for someone to match his strict criteria) leaps out in front of the frightened woman: "Hey, bitch, are you from California?"*
>
> *Frightened Damsel: "Nooo, Louisiana."*
>
> *Mr. Serial Killer: "Damn! Foiled again!"*

Obviously, the victims' looking alike may be more in the eyes of the press and public and not in the eyes of the serial killers themselves.

While it may be true that the killer has an "ideal" victim he's particularly attracted to, sometimes you have to settle for what's easy picking.

WHAT PHYSICAL CHARACTERISTICS OF A VICTIM ARE MOST ENTICING TO A SERIAL KILLER?

Pretty, if they can get 'em. As with choosing a mate, you like the healthy-looking pretty ones; they make lovely trophies. Teenage girls and young women are choice victims because of their lack of confidence and experience at fighting back (unless a serial killer picks a tough street girl, and he pretty much knows how not to do that). Besides, compared with older women, they are young, fresh and haven't "gone to seed" (SHE definition—grown tummies and developed thunder thighs through pregnancy and chocolate. SHE Note—dunno about you, not being the target of a serial killer because of a chocolate habit seems more of a perk than anything else).

Women who are small and easy to physically dominate are prime targets. If you're a welterweight you're not about to go and take on Mike Tyson, but you'll definitely consider a flyweight in high heels and a tight skirt.

> " *Q: What do you think when you see a pretty girl walking down the street?*
>
> *A: One side of me says, 'I'd like to talk to her, date her.' The other side of me says, 'I wonder how her head would look on a stick?'* "
>
> —EDMUND KEMPER

Elderly women are the one exception chosen by youthful offenders who lack experience and transportation. The little old lady living next door may be a fragile victim of osteoporosis and have some cash lying about the house; a piece of cake for the young wimpy serial killer (SHE Cheers—to the Senior Citizens who have fought back and kicked the daylights out of these guys).

WHICH WOMEN ARE IN THE MOST DANGER OF BEING ATTACKED?

Along with physical characteristics, the other determining factors for being chosen as a victim of a serial killer lie in vulnerability and the risks involved for the killer in grabbing that particular individual.

> "*People are like maggots: small, blind and worthless.*"
> —DAVID SMITH

At the top of the easy prey list are women no one knows have gone missing. Hitchhikers who thumb their way into extinction, prostitutes who haven't called home in a month anyway, and drug addicts who folks figure have run off with a good supplier don't set off alarm bells when they disappear. Because these women are not missed very quickly, the killer will not have to worry about an intensive investigation starting up any time soon. By the time the body of the victim is discovered skeletonized in a cow pasture in Idaho (SHE Terminology—Dead Woman in Field), identifying who she is and where she disappeared from is quite a chore. By the time that is accomplished, who the heck remembers who she was seen with a year ago.

Another reason these women are easy prey is that they just walk straight into the serial killer's trap.

"Wanna ride?"

"Fifty bucks?"

"Dime bag?"

It does not take a serial killer with great cleverness or social skills to master a two-word hook. Desperate women will get in a vehicle with anyone not waving a butcher knife in their direction at the time of the offer.

The next very vulnerable group of women is those who go to bars. They are a little riskier for the killer to grab because they will no doubt be missed in the next day or so. However, a woman who has been drinking will often go home with someone she shouldn't, or accept a ride from someone she doesn't know very well. If no one sees with whom she left, the serial killer knows there are no witnesses to identify him.

Women who insist on going to isolated places alone also put themselves at a much higher risk. Going for a jog on that lonely mountain path every day is a fine way to attract the attention of someone who may take note that your screams won't be heard once you are more than a hundred yards from the Ranger's station. Besides, when the passing "jogger" turns and whacks you over the back of the head with a club, you're not going to do a hell of a lot of screaming anyhow.

WHICH WOMEN ARE THE LEAST LIKELY TO BECOME VICTIMS?

Looking at physical characteristics first, overweight women and women who are strong and big boned are pretty darn safe! Serial killers simply don't want the risk of getting beaten up by a big woman, and overweight women are difficult to undress in a hurry.

This sounds terribly discriminatory, but reviewing the victims of serial homicide will reveal a pattern of smallish women who make for quick and easy work (not to mention that a small body is a lot easier to transport, hide, and hack into itty-bitty bits). Usually when a large or heavy woman is found murdered, it is not a stranger homicide (yes, I know that "Buffalo Bill" liked size 14 women, but he's not real!).

> " *Most of the people at the ranch were just people you did not want, people that were alongside the road.* "
>
> —CHARLES MANSON

The types of women serial killers are afraid of are those women who exude confidence and pose a threat to the success of their "mission." A serial killer has an ample choice of victims, and he's not about to gamble away his opportunity by picking on someone bigger and braver than he is.

WHAT CAN I DO TO ENSURE THAT I WILL STAY SAFE?

Witnesses, witnesses, witnesses. If you are every serial killer's wet dream, your best bet for personal safety is to resort to the ancestral behavior of traveling in packs. Simply never give him an opportunity to get you alone.

A woman's natural urge to go to the bathroom "in herds" is a primal instinct to protect her from attack. When you are most vulnerable, having the company of another woman offers the safety of numbers. Not just heading to the powder room, but going outside to have a smoke and walking to your car are really good times to not be alone as well.

This is not as oppressive as some will protest. Jogging around a popular park at a busy time of day works as well as going jogging on a path with fifteen of your closest friends. Serial killers don't abduct victims from public places with lots of people; they might be seen, and that ruins the whole plan.

> *When I murdered my wife I removed the one obstacle which for ten years had apparently held me in check. After she had gone the way was clear for me to fulfill my destiny.*
>
> —JOHN CHRISTIE

To those feminists who would like to yell and scream at me for promoting these safety tips instead of saying, "As a woman you have every right to _____", I would like to offer the following bit of advice. Your rights are not the ones in question—it's what he thinks his rights are. Besides, it's better to be safe than dead.

ARE MEN VICTIMS OF SERIAL KILLERS?

> *"He started messing with the Christmas tree, telling me how nice the Christmas tree was. So I shot him."*
>
> —*DAVID BULLOCK*

It does happen. A lot more often than people think.

Often serial homicides of men go unlinked. Gay guy stabbed in his own home. Gay guy stabbed in his own home. Gay guy stabbed in his own home—hm, must be a bad relationship thing. Society is still a little homophobic. We like to think we're open-minded and accepting of the homosexual lifestyle, but when it comes to serial homicide, we still lean on old stereotypes. Because much of society views a homosexual sexual encounter and relationship as weird or perverted, believing that a gay man would meet his end at the hands of his freaky lover makes sense. However, gay relationships are much the same as straight relationships. Some work, some don't, some are violent…. but a whole lot of dead gay males in a short time period or in a relatively small geographic area means a serial killer is most likely at work.

Do gay killers kill gay men?

Unless these are hate crimes, yes. However, the gay serial killer is not targeting gay men because he hates his own sexuality or is somehow anti-gay. He chooses his victims in much the same way and for the same reasons as the heterosexual serial killer. Straight serial killers choose women because to him they represent the society he has failed in. Killing women is a way to get back at everyone in it and get power on his terms. Gay serial killers want success within their world. Having failed to do well in this subculture, they target those who represent what they wanted and didn't manage to get. The homosexual male is a loser in his world, just as the heterosexual male is a failure in his.

One other reason for gay serial killers to target other gay males is simply the fact that they are easily accessible victims. The straight killer picks up prostitutes, women in bars, and uses ruses such as singles ads to obtain victims; gay killers use exactly those same methods. Likewise, the physical characteristics of victims of gay serial killers are similar to straight killers: small and easily handled. Gay serial killers want to be winners too and pick only victims who ensure the success of their mission.

Are straight men ever victims of serial killers?

Yes, there are non-homosexual victims of gay or bisexual serial killers. These tend to be young male hitchhikers and young men seeking work. John Wayne Gacy and Clifford Olsen are two of the worst offenders. Olsen offered rides to young people of both sexes. Both offered young men and teenagers (small and easy to control) employment and then alcohol and straight pornography to get their guard down. It isn't so much that these serial killers cared about the sexual orientation of their victims, but they were posing as purely heterosexual members of their communities and didn't want to blow their cover by involving themselves in openly gay activities.

Do heterosexual serial killers ever kill heterosexual men?

Although this happens much less often, it certainly does occur. In these instances, the sexual component of the kill is not present, but the issue of power still is. Sometimes the victim simply irritates the serial killer and he offs him just for the heck of it. Other times the victim is incidental to another crime like robbery or carjacking, especially for a serial killer on a spree.

Finally, sometimes you just have to get rid of witnesses. You want the girl, but her boyfriend came along for the ride. Shoot him and then go on and have your fun.

WHY WOULD A SERIAL KILLER CHOOSE CHILDREN FOR VICTIMS?

Children are small and portable, they are easy to dominate, and they pretty much do what a grown-up tells them to. This makes our kids prime targets not only for pedophiles, but also for serial killers.

Finding the right child victim is not difficult: shopping centers, at the playground, on the walk to school, or playing right outside in their own yards. Even if kids are in the company of other children, it's hardly a problem.

> *" I'm glad they caught me, because I'd do it again."*
> —ARTHUR GARY BISHOP

Working up a lie good enough to fool a thirty-year-old businesswoman takes a bit more sophistication than the lie it takes to snare an eight-year old. The "hardest" part of the crime is capturing the child (scary idea, huh?). From there, it's a matter of turning his fantasy into reality.

There are three types of child-killers. The most commonly thought of is the pedophile. Defining the pedophile is actually a lot more complicated than just saying "someone who likes to have sex with kids." While that is part of the definition, it's not the only part. There are those rare few true pedophiles that are sexually attracted to children; it is their sexual orientation. Then there are those who are attracted to the power—the idea that they are seen as an all-knowing authority figure—a task that's a lot easier to accomplish with kids than grown-ups. It is not like a pedophile to tear a child off of the street; he will build a relationship based on trust and authority. These men are spineless cowards and not likely to become serial killers. They will, however, kill in rare instances of panic when they are worried that their victim will expose them.

Serial killers who lack the social skills or physical strength to handle an adult will often resort to children. They have the pressing urge to kill but are unable to work up the courage to take on an adult. Robert Black seemed to have a vagina obsession with little girls, leading many to conclude erroneously that he was a pedophile. In actuality, he simply lacked the social skills and physical strength (read: wimp) to tackle a full-grown woman. Had Black been able to muster the courage, he most certainly would have committed his same sadistic acts on adult women.

Sometimes out of necessity the cowardly child-killer will have to gather that courage and resort to murdering teenagers or adults if there are reasons children become unavailable as victims. This is seen very clearly in the case of Wayne Williams. Working in Atlanta, Williams started with quite young children and teenagers, but when the body count became overwhelming, community vigilance increased, and the risk of getting caught abducting children became too high. He then picked his victims from socially disenfranchised men, homosexual prostitutes, drug addicts, criminals, and the mentally retarded and emotionally disturbed. He moved from high-risk to low-risk victims in order to continue his hobby without fear of arrest.

Then you have killers who, for lack of better victim, will take a child. This is the killer who prefers adult women but in a bind will take a pre-teen if that is all that is available. This killer is the rarest of child-killers (if you can call them that), and the victim is not so much targeted as they are convenient.

DO SERIAL KILLERS KNOW THEIR VICTIMS?

Okay, let's pick apart the word "know."

If we decide "know" means a long-term relationship (family member, spouse, significant other, neighbor or coworker) then the number of victims who "know" their killer is very tiny. Serial killers don't want to get caught. If everyone in the family ends up dead but you, folks might catch on and realize something is amiss. Soon, the police cars show up and you have some 'splaining to do.

> " *I love to kill people. I love watching them die. I would shoot them in the head and they would wiggle and squirm all over the place, and then just stop. Or I would cut them with a knife and watch their faces turn real white. I love all that blood.* "
>
> —*RICHARD RAMIREZ*

On occasion, an early victim of a serial killer is someone they know well who is very easy to access. Karla Homolka accidentally killed her sister Tami with an overdose of veterinary drugs she had administered so her boyfriend could rape the girl. From there, this vicious couple moved on to abducting and killing local girls.

Most of the time serial killers are smart enough to make sure it isn't too easy to connect the dots. Homolka and Bernardo knew picking another victim from their personal circle would cause people to think two dead acquaintances were a little too coincidental, so they went on to killing strangers.

A stranger homicide is the safest bet. Bop and dropping joggers, abducting women from parking lots, breaking into their homes—these victims leave the police totally clueless as to suspects because there doesn't seem to be any connection between the dead woman and her killer.

Now there are a number of women who are victims of serial killers they think they know. Suppose you are talking to a man in a smoky bar for three hours over beers—do you know him? If you went to high school together and you haven't seen him in twenty years—do you know him? If he is the produce guy where you shop—do you know him? If he's the guy you've gone out with twice—do you know him?

The truth is, not really.

Many serial killers select their victims from their daily haunts. This gives them time to observe and select a victim of choice and to establish just enough of a relationship to get her from point A to point B (from a safe place to an unsafe place) without her realizing she is about to become a victim.

Because the serial killer is not seen leaving with the victim, the fact that she does know him goes unrecognized. If he is seen with the victim, the fact that she does know him often eliminates him as a suspect! John Norman Collins admitted to police that he gave a ride to a coed who was found murdered, but he did not become a suspect because they didn't think a fellow student would kill her.

DO SERIAL KILLERS THINK THEIR VICTIMS DESERVE TO DIE?

Absolutely. How else can you justify killing and feel good about it? If being a woman isn't a good enough reason (Women are bitches and the world could use less of them), serial killers will invent something (The bitch insulted me).

Not only do serial killers feel their victims deserve to die, but they are darn proud to be their executioners.

> " *The women I killed were filth—bastard prostitutes who were littering the streets. I was just cleaning up the place a bit.* "
>
> —PETER SUTCLIFFE

THERE ARE NO VICTIMS, ONLY VOLUNTEERS

How serial killers choose their prey

<u>DO SERIAL KILLERS HAVE A PREFERRED HUNTING GROUND?</u>

Just like a hunter, serial killers pick locations where the prey they desire can be found. Depending on their skills and weapons, they will hunt their quarry in a manner, time, and place that ensures a successful hunt.

> *" Hurry it up, I could hang a dozen men while you're fooling around. "*
>
> —CARL PANZRAM
> *(FINAL WORDS PRIOR TO EXECUTION)*

The availability of a vehicle can be one limiting factor in choosing locations. Young adults often hunt close to home because they lack mobility. Serial killers who depend on public transportation kill near home, work and bus or subway stops.

Comfort is an important factor in the locations serial killers choose to conduct their hunt. A poor boy from a tenement slum is not going to be confident and comfortable stalking girls in Beverly Hills. He also is going to be very noticeable.

Probably someone will call the police to come and check him out. Likewise, a rich boy from Brentwood is going to be a tad conspicuous in the projects. He will be lucky if he doesn't become a victim before the day is out.

Blending in is extremely important. When a victim goes missing and the police start interviewing, it does not serve the killer well to be identified as the only out-of-place person on the block. One method of blending in used by killers is to patronize a place long enough to lose the "new guy" stigma. People don't expect people they "know" to be killers. So down at Benny's Bar, whatshisname becomes good ol' Larry, the harmless regular who is a little cheap in the tipping department. "Why, he's been coming here for a month and this is the first time anyone has come up missing, so it couldn't be him."

Blending in is less important when you can hide behind a tree by a pathway or behind a truck in the parking lot. Another simple trick is to simply get off the bus behind your victim. Chances are you won't be seen or remembered. Serial killers who use these methods may or may not have problems with social interaction. While it is true some lack the ability to lure their victims into a trap, others simply like the cheap thrill of jumping out at people or sneaking around in the dark. Not to mention you don't need to spend money buying broads drinks or waste money on clothes for the occasion.

Some serial killers hunt victims in their own homes. Single women without big dogs make great targets. The killer doesn't necessarily need a vehicle as he can take public transportation to the victim's neighborhood and return the same way. Some killers like the victim's home because they have more time to enjoy the crime and also get a few baubles to take home with them.

Sometimes serial killers don't work all that hard at hunting their prey. They just nab their victims wherever they cross their path. In the course of a year, a killer is bound to get lucky once or twice. Women just walking down a street, women staying alone in hotels, women who have car trouble, women with their hands full of groceries in a dark parking lot.... Anytime a woman gets separated from the herd, a predator may jump on the opportunity.

DO SERIAL KILLERS STALK THEIR VICTIMS?

Only as much as is necessary to get the job done. Sometimes they troll for hours, days, and weeks to find a good opportunity, and other times a handy victim falls into their lap.

> "*Dad, the world is getting darker now. I can feel it more and more...The girls call me ugly and they bother me the most.*"
>
> —DAVID BERKOWITZ

Most serial killers don't reach a level of stalking equal to that of a "real stalker" (SHE definition—an obsessed individual who feels a need to control a specific person). Serial killers just aren't that interested in anyone's life except their own. A stalking mentality at least requires the acknowledgement that the victim has some value, if only to be the object of one's obsession. A serial killer is only interested in a body that screams.

> "I always had the desire to inflict pain on others and to have others inflict pain on me. I always seemed to enjoy everything that hurt. The desire to inflict pain, that is all that is uppermost."
>
> —ALBERT FISH

WHAT KIND OF RUSES AND CONS DO SERIAL KILLERS USE TO GET VICTIMS?

Most ruses and cons are one-liners.

"Can I help you carry your bags? (to your deserted vehicle or empty apartment)

"Can you help me carry my bags? (to my deserted vehicle or empty apartment)

"Can I give you a ride?" (to a large open field)

"Can I help you fix your tire? (and hit you over your head with the lug iron?)

"I am here to fix your phone." (and wrap the cord around your neck)

"Can I use your phone? There's been a terrible accident." (and you're next)

"Wanna see my puppies, little girl?"

Some think that a serial killer who uses a ruse and a serial killer who uses a "blitz attack" (SHE definition—a sudden, violent attack) are always separate things. While some killers use a ruse to gain control of a woman and then continue the assault by controlling the woman with a knife, gun, or fear, others immediately render her unconscious as soon as she is within range.

"Candygram!" (Whack!)

Some don't even bother with the one-liner and just knock.

Fancier ruses play more on the victim's emotions and require a little more planning and a higher-quality act. Props bolster some of these cons: fake IDs, phony business cards, "police" badges, etc. The set-up requires some sort of scenario that will interest the victim to the point where she will go with the serial killer willingly. Some serial killers have posed as photographers. They play on a young woman's vanity and her desire to become famous. The serial killer shows her his "credentials" and offers to photograph her for free at his "studio" (read: van with no windows). All excited, off she goes, never to be seen alive again.

Some serial killers advertise through the personals. This has become increasingly popular in recent years. Newspaper ads, phone dating, and Internet singles sites make a cheap and easy way for serial killers to connect with women and set up a meeting. Using a phony name and a pager, the meeting is set up and the woman disappears.

Advertising items in the want ads can work both ways. Serial killers peruse the ads and call women to discuss the item for sale. If she makes the mistake of indicating that her husband is not at home—lo and behold, this is the only time frame he has available to check out the merchandise, and lo and behold, she ends up dead.

Sometimes a killer will advertise items himself and wait for the fly to come into his parlor.

A very popular con is the serial killer who sets up an appointment to view an empty house with a female real estate agent. This has been used enough times that real estate agencies are now taking better precautions before allowing women to go alone to show houses with a prospective male buyer. One safety measure is to make a copy of his driver's license before the agent goes out, but a copy of a phony license really doesn't provide much in the way of safety.

HOW OFTEN DOES A SERIAL KILLER "BOP-AND-DROP" HIS VICTIM?

"Bop-and-drop" serial killers (SHE definition—killers who hit victims over the back of the head or any other maneuver that renders the victim unconscious quickly) don't waste time with words. Hiding in bushes or coming up behind joggers as they run, the bop-and-drop eliminates the need for a con.

Bop-and-drop also eliminates the need to control the victim. With one quick whack on the skull or a punch to the face (or quickie stab to the chest or rapid throat slash from behind) the victim is down and pretty much out of it, preventing the victim from being pesky and fighting back. If the killer is able to effectively subdue the victim quickly, he also reduces the possibility that he himself will be injured. A victim who is still even semi-conscious will fight to save her life; and although she is likely to lose in

> *In the morning he was lying dead on one of the beds fully clothed. He was dead. I got the impression he wanted to go, and I must have killed him. I can't remember strangling him. I just sat there shocked.*
>
> —DENNIS NILSEN

these situations, the serial killer can't afford to leave an evidence trail. It's really easy to spot the guy with clawed-out eyeballs in the bar the next day; likewise, matching his fractured smile to the tooth fragments imbedded in her knuckles is a piece of cake.

The serial killer uses the bop and drop because it is quick, effective and leaves the victim in a state where she's easy to control, with no need to sweet-talk her. With today's forensic technology, the killer who leaves behind a drop of blood, a strand of hair or a few flakes of skin for a forensic team to find is setting himself up to be crucified in a court of law.

Serial killers do not necessarily pick just one method of getting their victims. A bop-and-dropper may work a particular ruse at times, while a ruse killer may get lazy and do a bop-and-drop. Serial killers that exclusively use bop-and-drops because they lack social skills may "move up" to cons as their human interaction improves (often after being involved in group therapy in prison or mental institutions).

It is also important to remember that just because a serial killer bops-and-drops does not necessarily mean he is afflicted with stuttering or has the face of a monster. This old profiler's tale theorizes that the killer is afraid to face his victim. In reality, some serial killers just like to nail 'em quick.

DOES A SERIAL KILLER FANTASIZE ABOUT HIS CRIME BEFORE DOING IT?

Sometimes serial killers will try to pull the wool over our eyes and say, "For no reason at all, I attacked the woman," or "Suddenly, this crazy idea just popped into my head and I found myself raping the woman."

Yeah, right.

When was the last time you just suddenly found your-self having sex with the mailperson in the middle of the street or stabbing the guide dog of a blind person as he rounded the corner?

> *"I haven't blocked out the past. I wouldn't trade the person I am, or what I've done—or the people I've known—for anything. So I do think about it. And at times it's a rather mellow trip to lay back and remember."*
>
> —TED BUNDY

Any time that you are the attacker in a brutal situation, there is an element of fantasy. You must somehow stage in your mind your actions, how the victim will react, and what the series of events is going to be. Without doing this, your chances of "winning" the confrontation are nil. There is always thought before action; however, from the victim's standpoint, there is not always time for thought before reaction.

To some degree, serial killers have not only fantasized their crimes, but rehearsed them many times before they actually attack; working out social situations, people's natural response and the physical requirements of committing their crime.

> *"Sex is one of my downfalls. I get sex any way I can get it. If I have to force somebody to do it, I do...I rape them; I've done that. I've killed animals to have sex with them, and I've had sex while they're alive."*
>
> —HENRY LEE LUCAS

DO SERIAL KILLERS ALWAYS CAREFULLY PLAN THEIR CRIMES?

Only if they have a reason to.

A sexually sadistic serial killer is planning to abduct a young woman and take her to his dungeon (read: basement his wife isn't allowed to go into) and torture her for days on end. He may spend as much time agonizing over details as a bride planning her wedding. And just like a bride who finds her happy day marred by a drunken groom, rain, and obnoxious guests, a serial killer may be less than satisfied with the actual results of his sexual homicide. He will then fantasize about the next time, making adjustments and perfecting his plan.

In order to plan and visualize his next kill, the killer may use ideas and images from books, movies, magazines, and the Internet. Like searching for new recipes in *Gourmet* magazine, a killer who wants to put together a really cool crime (usually a sexual sadist with a more complicated scenario) may borrow ideas from various sources. No one source is a "bible" for serial killers, nor is any true crime book or magazine going to provide the serial killer with a step-by-step plan.

Not all killers spend a lot of time planning their crimes. Sorting out what is necessary to commit a simpler sexual homicide can pretty much be figured out without a whole lot of input. Some things just come naturally to these folks, and a bop-and-drop kill isn't rocket science.

The FBI has labeled these two opposites as organized killers and disorganized killers. The theory is that the crime is supposed to represent the killer's level of intelligence and his ability to plan and carry out a series of specific actions. While there is some degree of comparison between how an individual handles a crime scene and how he handles his life, questions arise as to how much of what occurs at the crime scene is connected to the killer's preferences and emotional/psychological needs and what he was able to accomplish in a less-than-ideal situation (it's like planning a dream vacation, something always goes wrong).

Because these labels can't be applied absolutely, the FBI added the category of mixed (read: we can't really tell and we don't want to admit it).

Sometimes after a serial killer has committed a number of sexual homicides and the boys in blue haven't come knocking at his door, he no longer feels he has to be so careful and becomes sloppy. After all, why work harder than you have to?

WHAT SETS OFF A SERIAL KILLER?

> *" I didn't want to hurt them, I only wanted to kill them. "*
> —DAVID BERKOWITZ

Failure.

Serial killers are egotistical bastards who hate to fail. Unfortunately, because of their personality defects, they do it all the time. With as many failures as he has with women, work, money and overall respect, it's a good thing that they don't rush out to kill with every disaster. This is not necessarily because they're trying to be nice boys—strong law enforcement, financial constrictions and simple lack of opportunity may offer an ounce of prevention.

However, when the serial killer loses face in a particularly bad situation, suffers more than one failure at the same time, or one of the factors keeping him on the straight and narrow vanishes (like Mom dies), then he may feel the need to kill to get back the power and control he feels he has lost.

HOW CLOSE TO HOME DO SERIAL KILLERS GET THEIR VICTIMS?

Usually pretty darn close!

Many serial killers grab their first victim within one mile of home. With a first crime, the soon-to-be serial killer is going to be quite nervous. Therefore, he is going to want to control the variables as much as possible and kill where he is most comfortable. He may even just walk to the location, either because he has no car or because he is killing so close to home he doesn't want half the neighborhood to identify his car leaving the scene.

> " *It wasn't as dark and scary as it sounds. I had a lotta fun...Killing somebody's a funny experience.* "
> —ALBERT DE SALVO

Subsequent crimes tend to be committed within ten miles of home (not necessarily the same home, but wherever he is living at the time). Since people employed in menial jobs tend to work and play relatively close to home, crimes are often committed somewhere en route to these locations.

(SHE hot tip—Need a suspect? Start canvassing the neighborhood.)

One group of serial killers that falls outside of this range includes men who drive for a living. Truckers, delivery guys, taxi drivers and police officers may be more comfortable with their driving routes and work territories than their own residential neighborhoods. Therefore, they may kill on the job or drive their own vehicle back to an area they are very familiar with.

John Gerard Schaefer was a police officer in Florida who grabbed teenage girls in the middle of his workday. He tied them to trees, went back to work and then returned to rape and kill them. Not only was being a police officer handy in obtaining victims, but he had a seemingly good alibi that he "was at work" (as a police officer!) when the girls disappeared.

WHAT WEAPONS DO SERIAL KILLERS PREFER?

Supporters of the Second Amendment can breathe a sigh of relief.

Serial killers aren't usually particularly keen on guns. (David Berkowitz is one exception — he turned to using a gun after his knife attack on a victim failed dismally. Serial killer team John Allen Muhammad and John Lee Malvo are another exception to the rule, as Muhammad had a major obsession with commando operations and assault rifles). Up close and personal weapons: hands, knives, and bludgeoning tools are the favorites. These weapons actually frighten most victims more than the flash of gunmetal. Many serial killers and rapists have reported on the intimidation factor that a knife offers that a gun simply lacks; they believe that the victim is more afraid of a knife because she may live horribly disfigured. Even if he uses the gun to initially gain control of his victim, he will rarely use it to kill the victim.

> "It was as easy as taking candy from a baby. I remember thinking, 'You will have no more troubles, squire.' I felt I was doing him a favor. I felt his life was one long struggle."
>
> —DENNIS NILSEN

Another reason these weapons are favored is that a good part of the fun of serial killing is the primal urge of ripping apart your victim by your own physical prowess. This conquest over the victim makes the serial killer feel very strong and powerful. Never mind that he doesn't play fair and employs sneak attacks, uses a weapon when she doesn't have one, or picks victims that he can hardly lose to. This is pretty much equal to the sport of shooting fish in a barrel, but it still has the power to make a wimp feel God-like.

Addressing the issue of women who kill children, they tend to use "soft" methods like smothering and drowning. Using these methods, a woman can almost convince herself that the child just passed away. These women are not so much getting a thrill out of the kill as they are getting a thrill out of the results. In these cases, homicide can be difficult to determine. Many times the signs of smothering are overlooked, and the death is labeled a result of SIDS. A child drowned in the bathtub may be considered an accident unless there is something to prove otherwise.

Either mothers or nurses may administer lethal amounts of drugs. A misuse of a prescription drug is sometimes hard to detect, and if no one specifically looks for it, the cause of death may be brushed off as something like kidney failure. The true cause of death will be unknown.

Doctors and society are reluctant to accuse mothers of killing their children, and therefore a great many of these serial killer moms and nurses get away with their crimes. They usually are not caught until the number of deaths is so high that there is no explanation left except homicide.

WHAT TIME OF DAY DO SERIAL KILLERS TEND TO COMMIT THEIR CRIMES?

We tend to think that we are in the most danger of becoming a victim at night. There are certain populations of women that become more vulnerable at night:

> " *I'll kill the first man that bothers me.* "
> —CARL PANZRAM

prostitutes on the stroll, women drinking in bars, women walking through dark parking lots to their cars, night workers walking on empty streets or getting off buses at lonely stops, and women living alone asleep in their beds. Night certainly does offer serial killers many fine opportunities; therefore, a good many crimes do happen after dark.

However, dusk and dawn are a couple of times a day that catch women off-guard. We tend to think if it is still light or if it is getting light, we are safer. This is a prime time for serial killers to target joggers. There are few people out at that time on the paths and streets, and the killer does not have to worry about witnesses. Because of the false sense of security the victim has given herself, she may be less cautious of her surroundings and do things that are less than intelligent.

The middle of the day with the sun overhead also tends to make women feel safe. This is the time of day they think is okay to walk down country lanes and through natural parks.

The only difference the time of day makes in these locations is that during the day the killer can see what he is doing better. Heading to secluded areas alone is basically a bad idea any time of day.

It is also important to remember that if he's using a con, these little tricks work any time of day. They may even work better in the middle of the day, when the woman is feeling safe and secure.

Day or night, it is important to remember that if no one can see you, no one can see your killer with you either.

THE ACT

What happens during the crime

Do serial killers always rape when they kill?

Nope, but this doesn't mean it isn't still a sexual homicide.

Just because there isn't an actual rape doesn't mean there isn't a sexual assault. This could come in the form of oral sex, masturbation, touching, or object insertion. The offender may not commit a rape simply because this is not the kind of sex he likes, or he is afraid of AIDS, or he doesn't want to leave evidence.

> **"*Killing prostitutes had become an obsession with me. I could not stop myself. It was like a drug.*"**
>
> —PETER SUTCLIFFE

Some killers don't even bother with clearly sexual behavior at the scene. The killing itself may bring them to orgasm, or they may return home and masturbate as they play back the crime in their head. Some killers have been known to return to a crime scene to masturbate well after the crime is committed. To the serial killer, power is the ultimate aphrodisiac; in turn, they see sex as power. Intertwined, power and sex bring excitement and orgasm, and it is not necessary to have an actual sexual act to bring sexual gratification.

It's also important to note that serial homicide doesn't even have to mean sexual homicide. Women who kill children, nurses and doctors who kill patients, and black widows who kill off their husbands get off more on the power and attention than the sexual effects.

HOW CAN IT BE SEXUAL HOMICIDE IF THERE ARE NO SIGNS OF SEXUAL CONTACT?

Part of the reason was stated in the last question. As long as the serial killer gets sexual gratification from the homicide (during or after), then it is a sexual homicide.

The term 'sexual homicide' should be applied to the motive behind the kill. While the killer may never have any sort of sexual contact with the victim, that doesn't mean he's not getting off on it. If he's aroused by her posed dead body and sits back and masturbates while looking at her, is the crime any less sexual than if he raped her?

The other part of this answer lies in the fact that while there may be no evidence of sexual contact, certain sexual behaviors leave no mark on the victim. Gentle touching, masturbation, and nonviolent oral sex (either given or received) leave no evidence of sexual assault. Even sexual intercourse itself can be difficult to prove if the actual act did not cause any abrasions or damage. Some experts claim that any sexual act that is not desired by the victim leaves damage. The theory is that without arousal, there is no normal human sexual response that allows for penile penetration without causing harm to the woman's private parts. While this sounds pretty reasonable, it simply doesn't take into account a number of factors. First of all, the woman may have a

> "I had an unspeakable delight in strangling women, experiencing during the act erections and real sexual pleasure...It never occurred to me to touch or look at the genitals. It satisfied me to seize the women by the neck and suck their blood."
>
> —VINCENT VERZENI

reasonable amount of lubrication already present prior to the attack. Secondly, the killer may use some form of lubrication to help the act along. And, although guys don't like to admit it, some men are just kind of small down there and the woman might hardly notice he is raping her. Lastly, quick ejaculation may end the act before the woman suffers much in the way of noticeable damage.

Lack of semen at the scene also does not mean there was no sex. Using a condom (which is getting much more common these days among serial killers to protect against leaving evidence or getting a disease), doing a thorough clean-up job, and ejaculating somewhere else (off into the bushes, into a cloth or into his clothing), are a few effective ways to not leave semen for the cops to find.

DO ALL SERIAL KILLERS TORTURE THEIR VICTIMS?

While most serial killers get sexually aroused during a violent assault on the victim, which may or not include sexual acts, not all of them are practicing sexual sadists (SHE definition—they get sexually aroused by purposefully doling out pain or humiliation through perverse and painful sexual acts).

> *"I told one lady to give me all her money. She said no. So I cut her and pulled her eyes out."*
> —RICHARD RAMIREZ

While a "normal" serial killer might brutally beat, rape, strangle, and shove a tree limb into his victim, this is not the same type of behavior exhibited by the sexually sadistic serial killer. The latter keeps his victim alive for hours or days while he tortures her with all variety of sexually sadistic acts. He likes to see her pain, hear her screams, and make her beg and plead. He may have all manner of implements in his rape kit to accomplish the level of torture he wishes to achieve: whips, nipple clamps, X-acto blades, dildos, hot wax, enemas, garrotes, gags, and various bondage materials.

The goal is the same with both kinds of serial killers. They both want to exert power: one achieving power from the kill (a relatively quick process) and the other achieving power from the torture (as slow a process as he can make it) leading up to the kill.

DO SERIAL KILLERS COMMIT THEIR CRIMES THE SAME WAY EVERY TIME?

For some reason, when people hear 'serial killer' they assume that we are talking about a guy who commits the same crime over and over in the same way. Nothing could be further from the truth.

Media tries to convince us that the MO or Modus Operandi (SHE transla-

> *"I never knew where I was going, I never knew what I was doing—that's why you never nailed me... you never knew."*
>
> —ALBERT DE SALVO

tion—the basic necessities one needs to do to commit the crime) is static and that the killer will stick to this MO throughout his criminal career.

For example, a serial killer's MO might be that he abducts women from their cars in shopping center parking lots with a gun, takes them to a secluded park, ties them up, rapes them, strangles them with a cord, then leaves the bodies in the bushes. The car, the gun, the rope, the strangulation, and the dumping of the bodies are considered the things this killer must do to commit his sexual homicide. This, then, according to the static MO theory, is what he will do every time throughout his career.

Nonsense.

There are three reasons this is unlikely to be true.

It's boring. Nobody can do something over and over without becoming a little bored with the sameness. Even when a normal person has a particular favorite sexual fantasy with specific elements, he tends to change the characters, locations, and props just a bit each time to enjoy his particular fantasy with a fresh scenario.

A serial killer will do the same, adding or eliminating elements of his crime to suit his fancy. The popular notion that serial killers have some sort of obsessive-compulsive disorder (OCD) that causes them to kill over and over again like some programmed killing machine simply has no basis in fact.

Killers also tend to have moments of laziness and wild creativity. The killer who likes to con a woman into his van by asking her to help him change a tire might just get bored one day and whack a jogger on the back of the head with a two-by-four. Likewise, the cowardly bop-and-drop killer might try and convince his victim he's the telephone repair man and kill her in her own home.

Finally, there is a "natural progression" (SHE definition—learning and maturing; maturing and learning) of criminal behavior. Just as our budding serial killer began by experimenting with voyeurism and panty theft and then worked his way up to raping and killing, a new serial killer may only have simple elements in his first crimes, adding new twists as he gets older and more experienced. Of course, at times he may regress and go back to simpler methods, making his MO vary tremendously.

Gary Taylor is a great example of someone who seemed to change course constantly. He began his career by whacking women over the head at bus stops. Then he started shooting them with a rifle through their bedroom windows. He got caught and put away in a mental institution at this point. But when he was out on pass (after learning some good social skills), he posed as an FBI agent and obtained entrance to the victim's apartment. On the next pass, he bought some machetes and attacked women on the street. When he got out of the institution, he got married and (with more training in social skills from his wife), continued with a variety of ruses. After his divorce, he invited a couple of prostitutes to his house, where they ended up buried in his backyard. His ex-wife finally ratted him out, and when the police started hunting him, he reverted to a more bop-and-drop style, raping and not bothering to kill his victims.

So, folks, what is Taylor's MO? I haven't a clue!

To put it simply, an MO is what happened at that particular crime. If a number of homicides occur in the same area or within a short time frame that do have similar elements of MO, then certainly one might wonder if the same guy is committing these crimes. On the other hand, there are only so many ways to kill a person, so three bop-and-drop sexual homicides doesn't mean one killer did them all.

MO is one set of variables to be looked at when a series of sexual homicides occur. If one doesn't lock into the myths about MO, then the information gained by knowing how the killer operated at a crime can be compared with suspects and behaviors from other crime scenes and investigative avenues can be developed.

DOES A SERIAL KILLER LEAVE HIS "SIGNATURE" AT EACH OF HIS CRIMES?

The signature: A nifty little mystical notion that leads to the psyche of the serial killer—and the single biggest myth ever created by profilers and Hollywood about serial killers.

> " *That is my ambition, to have killed more people —more helpless people—than any other man or woman who has ever lived.* "
>
> —*JANE TOPPAN*

First, let's try to differentiate signature from MO (if we can). While an MO is defined as the elements of a crime necessary to accomplish it, the signature is supposed to be added touches that make the crime personal to the killer. Like the special brush strokes and color choices of an artist, there are special elements of the crime that are supposed to reflect the psychological makeup of the killer and positively identify the crime as his.

Hollywood usually portrays signature rather blatantly: diapers in the mouths of the victims, eyeball removal, a different biblical reference in every crime, or initials carved on the victim's forehead (BOB THE SERIAL KILLER WAS HERE). No doubt inspired by a few celebrity cases, actual blatant signature elements in serial homicides are rare.

Alberto DeSalvo, more popularly known as the Boston Strangler, would rape and strangle his victims and then leave them in provocative poses with the ligature he used to kill them tied in a pretty bow around their necks. Believe it or not, the bow and posing was a real-honest-to-goodness signature. He wanted to be certain to leave his calling card behind at every scene so the Boston Strangler would never go uncredited. For DeSalvo, it not only served the purpose of humiliation, but it also meant that he could bask in the glory of his infamy. For once, his pathetic existence demanded, if not respect, fear.

A dramatic signature makes for great movies and easy case linkage; in the real world, these signatures are the exception rather than the rule. For one thing, serial killers don't want to be caught and it doesn't pay to have crimes that are easily connected. Only a few, wanting to whip the public into a state of frenzy and watch the publicity, want the killings to be known as a series. Most killers simply don't care what the public thinks, and in the commission of their crimes, the only fear they're interested in is the intense and direct fear of their victim.

Profilers also talk a lot about signature—nothing quite as obvious as the Hollywood movies, but there is a strong belief that if the crime is analyzed carefully, a ritual can be found apart from the MO. This ritual, they claim, will remain constant from crime to crime—even if the MO changes. Unfortunately, much that is claimed to be signature is more the profiler's own take on what the killer's behavior means.

One example offered in the Crime Classification Manual (CCM) of the difference between MO and signature focuses on the behaviors of two rapists. One makes a woman's husband lie on the floor in the next room with a cup and saucer on his back and tells him, "If I hear that cup move or hit the floor, your wife dies." The other rapist ties the husband to a chair and forces him to watch. The CCM designates the first behavior (cup and saucer) as MO (to keep the husband under control so he could rape the wife), and the second behavior (force-husband-to-watch) as signature (a need to humiliate). However, who's to say Rapist Number One didn't get a sick kick out of thinking of the husband lying helpless and looking like an idiot with a cup-and-saucer on his back listening to his wife's screaming in the next room?

Going by profiler (not Hollywood) standards, the signature is far less obvious, and usually quite vague. The profiler might say that the signature of a serial killer is that he has a need to humiliate (as in the crime scene just mentioned), or he is excessively violent, or he has a need to insert objects into the victim's orifices. The problem with these signature groups is that they tend to be difficult to categorize (too many psychiatric designations), and they are often twisted to fit crimes that are unrelated.

Sexual serial killers really tend to come in only two varieties: the "normal" kind and the sexual sadist I mentioned a little earlier. These two designations cover the two methods of getting power through the sexual homicide. These methods are hardly signatures, because all sexual serial killers fall into one group or the other.

These are two fairly distinct groups of behaviors, and a serial killer rarely leaps from one to another. Most will stay put with one method of power attainment throughout their criminal history. However, this is not to say that a killer cannot get to a point where he finds his power method unsatisfactory and moves on to the other method.

But with the complicated signature method, profilers run into real problems trying to figure out a signature or trying to fit some of the killer's crimes into the pattern. So when signature becomes difficult to discern, the profiler says circumstances may have changed his normal behavior, or that the body is too decomposed to allow the profiler to identify signature. If the behavior changes dramatically but still has some similar elements, the profiler will call this "evolving." (Perhaps just the killer changing groups, or it could be that there are two killers with totally different game plans, and that is why it doesn't match.)

Often a profiler doesn't write his "profile" with the signature aspect until after the serial killer has been convicted of his crimes and has laid them out in detail for the profiler to analyze. Looking at anything in retrospect, one can easily "see" the similarities (and those that don't fit are just accidentally left out of the profile).

With only two basic groups of sexual serial killers—the "normal" serial killer and the sexually sadistic serial killer—the only way to link crimes further is to look at similar MO elements, locations, time between kills, and the suspects known to be in the area.

Discerning a "signature" in a crime makes a profiler look brilliant as he uses his specialized knowledge of serial killers and psychological analysis to "figure out who did it." This is quite ego-enriching for the profiler, but in reality, figuring out who committed the crime is really the result of an incredible number of investigative hours and teamwork putting together all the pieces of the puzzle.

WHY WOULD A SERIAL KILLER HAVE SEX WITH THE BODY AFTER THE PERSON IS DEAD?

It's the only way some of these guys can score. Only when the woman cannot reject his sorry self can he play with and explore her body without being told to take a hike.

"I took her bra and panties off and had sex with her. That's one of those things I guess that got to be a part of my life—having sexual intercourse with the dead."

—HENRY LEE LUCAS

Necrophiliac serial killers each seem to have a preference as to which specific post-mortem stage is his favorite for intercourse. Some prefer to rape their victims right after they die, so that she's "still warm" and feels almost as if she's alive. Others wait until she's dead long enough to be cold and rigor mortis has set in so that he knows she's dead (but still not stinky). Others prefer to wait until the corpse has had time to decompose as a final insult; others run the gamut and will rape the body any time he feels the need.

Like "regular" rape, post mortem rape is not so much about having sex as it is showing power over another person. Some killers are so hooked on the power of the kill that they cannot actually get aroused unless they have experienced the ultimate power of killing their prey. To them, killing is foreplay.

Power is sexy, and some guys find the ultimate power in causing death.

WHY DO SOME SERIAL KILLERS CHOP UP THE BODIES?

> *"They were dead and I was alive. That was the victory in my case."*
> —EDMUND KEMPER

It's a good way to get a very personal souvenir (a locket can be from anywhere, but a foot...). It's also one more way to show power. For Jerome Brudos, nothing said, "You're mine, baby" like a foot in the freezer. It was his way of possessing the victim even after he'd disposed of the rest of her body. Brudos had a propensity for feet, and in the early days of his foot fetish he collected shoes and stockings. By the time he had graduated to killing, it was only logical for him to want to have a lady's foot of his very own.

Even if you aren't collecting souvenirs, hacking somebody up can be a continuation of having power over the individual. One of the reasons many folks like an open casket viewing is because seeing the body gives them the feeling their loved one still exists in this world. Likewise, seeing a just-killed body nice and whole makes some serial killers feel like they haven't totally won the battle. Hacking the body into pieces makes the annihilation complete and the killer the total victor. He is now everything, and she is nothing.

Sometimes chopping up the body has nothing to do with a need for more power. The serial killer simply needs to get rid of the evidence. Suppose the killer murders a woman in his third-story apartment and the elevator in his crappy building has not functioned for a week. Not only that, his three-hundred-dollar car needs a new battery. It's awfully heavy and noisy to carry a body down three flights of stairs and rather conspicuous to carry it out the front door of the building in front of all the neighbors hanging out on the steps. Much better to hack her up and take her out in trash bags, section by section, and toss the bags in a dumpster down the block.

Getting rid of the body in parts also has the advantage of the homicide going undetected longer. As long as Cookie's body isn't found, it is just assumed she has moved or run away. The killer doesn't have to worry about the police nosing around and asking questions. If the body parts are found, the victim may be impossible to identify for a long time, and by the time the police figure out who it is, no one remembers much about her activities at the time of her disappearance.

WHY DO SOME SERIAL KILLERS EAT PARTS OF THEIR VICTIMS?

> **" I Bite. "**
>
> —*JEFFREY DAHMER*

Believe it or not, for some serial killers, murdering and chopping up the body is still not enough of a win! For these killers, it is the ultimate to be able to say, "Hah! Not only did I kill you, but I cut you into bits, cooked you for dinner, and chewed you up!"

Jeffrey Dahmer claimed eating his victims made him feel closer to them. It is hard to know how true this is. This statement did go along with his story of wanting to make zombies of the guys he brought home so they wouldn't ever leave him, but this is something from his own excusing state of mind, so he may have just said this to sound pitiful and not seem like such a bad guy.

Not to mention it's a great way to get rid of evidence. It's pretty hard to go chasing bits of digested people through the sewers. Killers who eat their victims for this reason tend to stick with those body parts that make victim identification easier.

WHY DO SOME SERIAL KILLERS POSE THEIR VICTIMS' BODIES?

It makes a nice display and prolongs their control over the victim. Not only that, the control then carries over to the person who finds the body and the police who come to the crime scene. And even better, the serial killer knows the police will take pictures of the crime scene and his work will be forever documented. A good pose will go a long way….

There are actually not many serial killers who go to the trouble of posing their victims. Most just leave their victims where they lay when they are finished with them. They lose interest in the body once they have finished killing the victim and go on their way. Some leave as quickly as possible so they aren't caught in the act, and others just leave because they're finished with their work and it's time to head home.

> **"With great sadness and remorse, I realize that I allowed myself to be misled by Satan."**
> —ARTHUR GARY BISHOP

On occasion, profilers have decided a body is posed when it's just flopped into a grotesque position. Other times it is very clear that the victim is posed. As can be noted in one of Danny Rolling's crimes, there is no way the victim's dismembered head just accidentally ended up on the furniture staring directly at the front door; it was placed there. Obviously, it tickled Rolling to imagine the look on the face of the first person to open the door and encounter this ghastly sight.

DO SERIAL KILLERS TAKE PICTURES OR VIDEOS OF THEIR KILLING?

> *" For me a corpse has a beauty and dignity which a living body could never hold... there is a peace about death that soothes me. "*
>
> —JOHN CHRISTIE

Many don't bother. Taking pictures of their assaults is not usually on their minds when they choose to do someone in. "Normal" killers are into rage and killing, not documentation.

This kind of behavior is more common with the sexually sadistic serial killer because he is so heavily into the elements of his torture scenario (and violent, hard-core pornography as well). He may well like to have his own personal pornographic collection of his victims in various poses and situations. With a picture, video, or audio recording, he can review his crime in living color and/or sound and enjoy himself tremendously between kills. Also, the action of taking photos, video, or taping the victim is an added humiliation that is sexually exciting to the killer.

Ian Brady and Myra Hindley fell in love over a copy of *Mein Kampf* and had romantic discussions about concentration camps. They quickly discovered they were both into bondage and torture. Brady and Hindley decided to extend their sadistic sexual rituals to the children they would abduct, rape, and kill. So they would never be without a fresh source of pornography, they carefully documented their kills with photographs and audio recordings so they would have plenty to keep themselves titillated.

There is one disadvantage for the killer in documenting his crimes: it makes for incontrovertible evidence in the court-room. Clearly, in spite of this possibility, the pros outweigh the cons from these killers' perspectives, because they quite arrogantly believe they are not likely to be caught anyway.

SMOKE A CIGARETTE

Post-offense behavior

DO SERIAL KILLERS KEEP SOUVENIRS?

Some but not all.

Taking a personal item from a victim allows the killer a little memento for him to get sappy about. Seeing the charm bracelet of your latest victim dangling from the wrist of your wife (you thoughtful boy!) gives the killer a dirty little secret to get turned on about. Killers have been known to keep (aside from body parts) pieces of jewelry, shoes, and undergarments for just these sentimental reasons.

> "*She insisted upon killing Lesley Ann Downey with her own hands, using a two foot length of silk cord, which she later used to enjoy toying with in public, in the secret knowledge of what it had been used for.*"
>
> —*IAN BRADY*

Some killers have admitted to the delight they got from keeping in public view the weapon with which they killed their victims. Using the rope he bound his victim with to tie down a load of rubbish for the dump brings him a whole new thrill. Here is evidence of his crime, right out in the open, and nobody has a clue.

Something else that I should point out here: while he may take the cheap sterling silver chain with the crystal angel on it for sentiment, he may also take the one-carat diamond ring to pawn so he can put gas in his van.

HOW DO SERIAL KILLERS CHOOSE WHERE THEY DUMP THE BODIES OF THEIR VICTIMS?

> " I should never have been convicted of anything more serious than running a cemetery without a license "
>
> —JOHN WAYNE GACY

First the serial killer must decide if it is worth his effort to move the body from wherever she was actually killed. Moving and dumping bodies is quite a bit of work, and carting them around in your vehicle is a good way to get nabbed for the crime (more than one serial killer has been stopped for a traffic violation and unable to give a good explanation for the body under the blanket in the back seat).

If leaving the victim in her own house or where she dropped on the bike path is not going to unduly point the police to the killer (he lives next door, or the path stops at his house), it may be easier not to bother moving the body.

The other reason killers move bodies is to slow down its discovery and allow time for evidence to be destroyed—one more thing a killer must consider when he makes his decision to leave or move a body.

Suppose he does decide to move the body from the location where the victim was killed. Take, for example, the serial killer who abducts a woman from the parking lot of the local food store. Driving a mile up the road to a picnic ground, he rapes and kills her there. He decides to dump her some place else so the police won't find the evidence of where he actually killed her. He tosses the body in the trunk of his car and drives off to find a better place to leave her.

At this point he must decide how quickly he wants the body to be found. If he isn't too worried about evidence, he may dump her on the side of the road where she will be found by morning. If he doesn't want the body discovered, he may work harder to find a spot in the woods where he can hide the body under some brush or toss it down a ravine. He may also choose to dump the body in a populated location, like the parking lot of an apartment building or an empty lot in the city—a good way to add a lot more suspects to the list.

In order to get away with dumping the body and not be seen doing it, a serial killer needs the ability to blend in with his surroundings. If he has chosen a spot way off the beaten path in the mountains, he doesn't have to worry much about being seen (but he does have to worry about getting stuck in the mud and needing to call a tow truck company to get him out).

Dumping the body on the side of the road is a little more risky. Other cars may whiz by as he is attempting to toss the body. However, if he just keeps his eye on the road, he can do each part of the task when no one is driving past him (open the trunk or door, toss the body behind the car where it is blocked from sight, jump in car and take off). Later, because nothing really suspicious was seen at the time, most passersby will have no memory of the event.

Leaving the body in a neighborhood is a little trickier. In order for the killer to sit for a bit in his vehicle waiting for an opportune moment, he must blend in well enough for the locals not to wonder what he's up to. It helps to be of the same race as the neighborhood residents and have a vehicle that matches the area as well. Only if there is an alley behind a building or large dark parking lot behind a set of apartments can a person who would normally stand out in the community take the chance of dumping a body in that location. On occasion, a killer will do just that, hoping to misdirect the investigation by making the police think the killer is of another race or social status.

DOES A SERIAL KILLER ALWAYS DUMP HIS VICTIMS' BODIES AT THE SAME LOCATION?

Suddenly there is a story in the newspaper about a serial killer in the area! Why? Because a number of bodies are found in one location at the same time.

> *"Every man to his own tastes...mine is for corpses."*
> HENRI BLOT

What usually happens is some poor sucker trips over a body as he is taking a stroll in the woods. ("What a lovely day! Listen to the birds singing, breathe the fresh air, look at that decomposed body...?!"). When the police show up and start looking around, one of the officers shouts "Over here! There's another one!" After a complete search of the area, some four or five bodies are discovered in different stages of decomposition, indicating they were killed and dumped at different times. Now the community pretty much knows there is a serial killer around, and the police have no problem linking the bodies together as the work of one serial killer. So why would the killer dump them all in the same spot?

Obviously, he had found a pretty good dumping ground. The serial killer dumped the first body and no one found it. Eureka! This is a good place to get rid of unwanted things. He simply keeps dumping the bodies there until his site is discovered. Then he moves on to another location.

Most serial killers dump in a variety of locations. That way the police and the community don't suspect a serial killer, and he can continue to operate without much trouble. He may even pick dump locations in different police jurisdictions to further keep the crimes from being linked.

DO SOME SERIAL KILLERS COMMIT THEIR CRIME AT ONLY ONE LOCATION?

> " *We wanted to do a crime that the world would have to stand up and take notice.* "
>
> —SUSAN ATKINS

Yes. The two kinds of homicides that tend to contain the crime at one location are those murders that occur in the victim's home and those that are bop-and-drops on paths. The number one reason for the rape and murder to occur at one spot with the body just left there is that the killer doesn't have a car to transport the body in. Therefore, he really doesn't have a choice in the matter. But even if he does happen to have a vehicle, he's going to get a lot more attention dragging his new friend through the park and hoisting her into the trunk than if he just bolts from the scene.

Also, as we stated in the previous question, if the killer isn't all that concerned about being identified, he may not worry about all that body dumping stuff. Besides, she's nothing but some worthless piece of trash; just leave her where she is.

"Dead weight" is another factor. Moving a body is a lot of work, and you're not going to get much in the way of cooperation from the victim. Even small bodies can be difficult to move by yourself—especially if Mr. Serial Killer isn't very big.

And, oh the mess! After Mr. Serial Killer has created a bloodbath by stabbing the victim seventy-six times, dragging her to some place he can hide her is going to be a bit foolish. He's going to leave a blood trail to follow—from the scene to his clothing to the trunk of his car to his residence—that is even worse than the blood trail he could possibly leave without handling the body any further. DNA from the victim's blood, when found on the killer's clothes, in his vehicle and home, is damning physical evidence the prosecution can use in court to nail the killer to the wall.

DO SERIAL KILLERS SHOW UP AT THE FUNERAL OR GRAVE OF THE VICTIM?

Wow, what a cliché. But ya' know, these stereotypes have to come from somewhere. Oddly enough, there are serial killers who do show up at gravesites and at the funerals of their victims.

> *"I talked to her saying I was sorry for what I had done. It was the first time I had apologized to someone I had killed."*
>
> —PETER SUTCLIFFE

However, it is more common with the first kill, when the victim is likely to be from the killer's immediate neighborhood or family, and his absence would be more of an alarm than his presence.

Some killers go to the gravesite after the funeral, perhaps as one last "Ha ha, you're dead and I'm not!" and occasionally leave items or steal things from around the headstone as a last-ditch effort to collect a souvenir.

Serial killers have also been known to return to the scene of the crime—but usually only if it is in a secluded or safe place. It allows the killer to extend his enjoyment of the crime a while longer and relive what occurred at the crime site.

On the other hand, you have those killers who are finished with their crime the minute the victim is dead or dumped and won't bother with either post-offense behavior (SHE definition—things criminals do after a crime).

DO SERIAL KILLERS KEEP A JOURNAL OR A SCRAPBOOK OF THEIR CRIMES?

This is the first time in their lives a lot of these serial killers have accomplished anything. Even though they are not identified by name in the newspaper articles, they know who did it; they know who the bad man really is. Some clip the articles and put them in a nice little book; some stick them on the walls of a private room, and others just stuff them someplace. If you have a relative who for no special reason has a collection of local homicide stories stashed somewhere, you might want to check and see if he has other issues as well.

> *"I stood there amazed. I found it all hard to believe, that I, Des Nilsen, had actually done all that."*
>
> —DENNIS NILSEN

Unlike photos of the actual body at the crime scene, news clippings are not proof that the person saving them had any connection to the death of the victims. He could just be a flaming weirdo with a fascination for homicides. However, while the clippings are not proof in a court of law, they can certainly be useful for trying to figure out who the other victims of the serial killer might be.

Some killers don't even bother to read the paper or watch the news. They simply go on their merry way and don't look back. This type of killer makes it harder for family members to realize they are serial killers, because they haven't left any evidence of their crimes (souvenirs or clippings) lying about. In fact, these killers may show so little interest in a murder in their own community, friends and family would find it hard to believe he could commit such a horrendous crime and be so totally blasé about it.

DO SERIAL KILLERS BRAG OR TALK ABOUT THEIR CRIMES BEFORE THEY ARE CAUGHT?

When a murder goes unsolved for a long time, it's common to hear that the killer must be dead, because if he were alive, he would have told someone about the crime by now. The logic here is a bit off. It isn't that the killer must be dead; it might be that he hasn't sent out a news bulletin about his crimes.

> *I would go home and watch what I done on the television. Then I would cry and cry like a baby.*
>
> —ALBERT DE SALVO

Some killers never tell a soul. Others allude to their crimes with cryptic messages like, "You don't know what I've done," or "Someone was murdered in that field."

Occasionally they claim a buddy has told them about some crime he committed, or describe the crime, replacing the victim of the homicide with himself as the victim of an assault or attempted suicide. These methods allow the killer to share the more interesting details with his audience without actually implicating himself.

Other killers ask their buddies to hide murder weapons or other pieces of evidence. John Norman Collins gave his friend a knife to hide when police learned he was the last person seen with a girl who had disappeared. One would think this guy would turn his butt in, but the friend was a criminal in his own right and didn't much like the police, so Collins wasn't being all that stupid.

Even when killers actually say, "I did it" to people, they may not believe him. When a loser whose biggest claim to fame is that he's held his last job for more than six weeks brags about being an infamous serial killer, it's a little hard to take him seriously. For every bona fide serial killer out there, you're likely to find at least a handful of serious losers willing to confess to a series of murders, even though they had nothing whatsoever to do with them.

WHAT DOES A SERIAL KILLER DO RIGHT AFTER THE CRIME?

> *"We've all got the power in our hands to kill, but most people are afraid to use it. The ones who aren't afraid control life itself."*
>
> —RICHARD RAMIREZ

He splashes cold water on his face, stumbles down the street in a stupor, then falls into a terrible depression and drinks himself into oblivion while babbling incoherently about murder to Steve the apathetic bartender—no wait, that's the profiler at the end of the workday.

The serial killer is off eating a hamburger and french fries.

While occasionally you'll find the killer who becomes moody, loses weight, and drinks a lot after he kills, most guys just go back to life as usual. A little bit of clean-up, a bite to eat and they're ready to go home and spend time with their wife and kids. It's important to understand that if a serial killer truly got depressed after a kill, it would be a lot easier to catch him—just look for the guy in the neighborhood who's about to jump off a bridge for being such a terrible monster. Instead, the serial killer shows up back at work and no one is any the wiser.

Any depression a serial killer might feel doesn't stem from feeling bad about what he's done; more often it's a feeling of inadequacy if his crime didn't exactly go according to plan, or worry that he's going to get caught. Instead of pondering "Was I being selfish to end the life of such a beautiful and vibrant woman?" he's more likely asking himself "Did I remember to wipe my prints off of the phone when I tore the cord out of the wall to tie her up?"

Next priority—sort out an alibi. The guy running to all his female relatives telling them "If anyone asks where I was tonight, tell them I was with you," should be suspect, as they usually do this long before the crime is announced publicly.

Although some serial killers may display nervousness for a few days after the murder, this behavior lessens dramatically after the first kill or two. Once the killer realizes he can get away with murder, he displays much more calm and arrogance.

HOW DO SERIAL KILLERS GET RID OF THE EVIDENCE?

Wash it away, wipe it off, take it away and dump it; burn it, bleach it, dissolve it, give it away, or bury it.

At the scene, if the killer has any smarts, he'll be sure to destroy any possible evidence he left. He needs to wipe off fingerprints and semen and wipe up any blood that is his. He might wash his hands off in the sink or even take a shower

> **"...There was some meat on the stove in a frying pan. I think it was human flesh. I...found her in my bathtub, and part of her buttocks was missing. The feet were gone, the hand, the arm. I found them in the refrigerator."**
>
> —EDDIE COLE

to get rid of blood on his hair or clothes before getting in his car or being seen elsewhere. He might destroy any footprints he has left and check to be sure he didn't drop his wallet at the scene.

If he's driving, he may head to a gas station and vacuum the car, wipe down the interior, and run the vehicle through the car wash.

Any evidence he took from the scene, any clothes he wore or any weapons he used that might lead the cops to him, he may toss in a dumpster or out in the woods. Sometimes the killer will burn, dissolve, or bury the evidence to make absolutely sure it will never resurface.

A few killers take a lot more risks and give the evidence to a friend (jewelry or a gun). Some pawn items, and those who really don't want to give the stuff up keep it in a storage locker.

DOES A SERIAL KILLER REPLAY HIS CRIME IN HIS MIND OVER AND OVER OR JUST FORGET ABOUT IT?

There are those moments in life that you see as your crowning glory, when you were King of the Universe—for some guys it's scoring the winning touchdown in a high school football game; for others, it's their war days; then you get the stray few who see their moments of triumph as hacking up a few frightened coeds.

Unlike the football star and war hero, the serial killer can't really ramble on at cocktail parties about his achievements (they have to wait until after they're in prison to do that). Knowing what he has done and not being able to openly brag about it is a difficult situation for the serial killer. As I mentioned before, while he may share information with a few select friends, and allude to the crimes to others, it's still not socially acceptable to go into the details of his kills with anyone who will listen.

In his mind, all the little things that went wrong with the crime quickly become fuzzy, and he soon has a perfect slasher movie in his

> " I remember, as I gazed down at the still form of my first victim, experiencing a strange and peaceful thrill. "
>
> —JOHN CHRISTIE

head about how great he was, how terrified she was, and how easy it was to kill her.

He lives on these fantasies, not necessarily until they wear out and he gets bored with them, but until he can convince himself he really is the perfect killing machine and can easily create another masterpiece of terror.

SMOKEY AND THE BANDIT

Catching killers

WHY ARE SERIAL KILLERS SO HARD TO CATCH?

Mainly because no one sees them commit the crime! This is the top reason why investigators can't just go arrest them in a day. With crimes of rage—barroom brawls, angry husbands and boyfriends, bad drug deals—at least you have

> " *You maggots make me sick. I will be avenged. Lucifer dwells within us all.* "
> —RICHARD RAMIREZ

suspects. There are often witnesses to these homicides; and when there aren't, there are at least pretty strong connections between the killer and the victim. All the investigators need to do is find the evidence and not blow the case by losing it or screwing up some legal technicality.

In sexual homicides, there are rarely any witnesses and the killer often has only a very slight connection to the victim. Even if he somehow gets on police radar, he may be interviewed by the investigators but crossed off the suspect list because he didn't seem like such a bad guy, or he had a "good alibi" (that someone didn't actually check out). Once he's off the suspect list, he may never be focused on again.

The next-most important factor in failing to catch serial killers is something called "linkage blindness" (SHE Definition—not realizing that two or more crimes may have been committed by the same person). As discussed before in the issues of MO and signature, it is often very difficult to decide if a series of homicides are connected. Many times if there is not some very obvious factor in the murders, they are just labeled as a one-off crime. This is especially true if there is no clear evidence of a sexual assault. Even if there are three bop-and-drop victims on bike paths in the same year, if they occur at different parks with somewhat different victims, maybe at varying times of the day, the police may just think there were three different killers. If a killer moves his crimes even a few miles, he may also be in a totally new police jurisdiction, where they have no knowledge of the crimes just a couple of minutes away. Especially when law enforcement is not looking for a serial killer, they are unlikely to communicate very well with those in another police department.

Serial killers also cannot be caught if there is not good physical evidence to take to court. Evidence is sometimes nonexistent. If the body of the victim stays hidden for a very long time (remains of "Dead Woman in Field"), salvaging any physical evidence from her remains is next to impossible. Other times the forensic procedure used in collecting the evidence is less than perfect (read: seriously messed up) and gets contaminated or destroyed. Likewise, if the case goes unsolved for a decade, the evidence may get lost, accidentally destroyed, or ruined in a flood or fire while it is sitting in an evidence box in some storage closet.

Even when the police are darn sure they have a serial killer and know who he is, if they lack the evidence to take him to court, his name will likely never be given to other police departments with similar unsolved homicides. He simply walks away into the community without a mark or note on his record.

IS THERE ALWAYS DNA EVIDENCE FOUND AT THE CRIME SCENE?

No, and it's getting harder and harder to win a court case without it.

Sometimes the serial killer simply doesn't leave any. If the kill is quick and there is no actual rape, he may not leave any semen or blood at the scene. Unless the victim's blood can be found on him or in his environment, there is no DNA connecting him to the scene.

> "I saw him...at peace in my armchair. I remember wishing he could stay in peace like that forever. I had a feeling of easing his burden with my strength."
> —DENNIS NILSEN

If the victim scratches the killer, she may have his skin under her nails and that can be tested for DNA. If the serial killer uses a condom, again he will leave no semen. Only if the condom is found and turned in to the police can it be tested for the victim's cells, which could provide a DNA link to the crime scene.

Other kinds of DNA can be gotten from the killer if he leaves saliva on the victim or on a cigarette butt found at the scene. Vomit also may have DNA in it (although it isn't very easy to extract the DNA from it), so if the killer threw up, there might be some evidence there.

It used to be that all forensic testing was based on what DNA could be collected from the nuclei of a cell—seriously limiting how much DNA you could actually extract from a sample of blood, hair or semen. With Mitochondrial DNA (mtDNA) it's a little different. MtDNA has the advantage of having hundreds of testable DNA molecules in any one cell. This kicked the evidence door wide open when testing bodily fluids that were previously of no use as DNA samples. Saliva, vomit, urine, and feces can now be carefully tested and DNA samples extracted—not necessarily from the fluid itself, but from trace elements of blood and skin that may be present—even if it's been sitting around for a while being mauled by the elements and time. So what's the problem with mtDNA testing? It's a very time-consuming, rigorous process and very few labs have the technology and experience to perform these tests (not to mention there are whole slews of medical examiners and investigators that have no clue that this testing is even available!).

Up until the development of mtDNA testing, the three tests that have been used for DNA analysis are RFLP, PCR, and STR. To put it in simplistic terms, RFLP requires a whole lot of DNA, PCR a puddle, and STR just a drop (but still more than mtDNA testing). Way back when, cases were tested with RFLP. When science got better, PCR was used, and now STR is the most common method. What this means is that we can now test much tinier amounts of DNA, so we can go back to old cold cases where no DNA was found because RFLP or PCR testing required too much, and we might now find DNA with the STR tests! This new technology is helping to close cases that before had no evidence to support them. Unfortunately, linking older cases with newer cases is a problem, because the older ones that had DNA from RFLP and the newer ones tested with PCR or STR can't be compared—the results from the tests can't be matched.

IS THERE EVER A CRIME SCENE WHERE NO EVIDENCE IS FOUND FROM THE KILLER?

Unfortunately, yes.

It is hard to believe that a killer could rape and murder someone and not leave any trace of himself at the scene. Locard's Exchange Principle Theory (SHE definition—You can't go

> "*I will in all probability be convicted, but I will not go away as a monster, but as a tragedy.*"
>
> —JOEL RIFKIN

somewhere without leaving a bit of yourself behind and taking a bit of the place with you) is just that—a good theory. In reality, sometimes you just can't find anything. Along with not leaving DNA, it is also possible that the killer's hair didn't get ripped out or fall out during the attack (or he may have worn a cap or he may have been totally bald). He may have worn gloves so he left no fingerprints. Some killers remove their shoes so they don't leave shoeprints.

Then they may have cleaned up the scene darn well before they left, or the killer might have dumped the body in the stream and all the evidence washed away.

Sometimes the fault lies with the collection of the evidence. After it is done completely incompetently, the police department may simply say there was no evidence at the scene. After all, doing sloppy work is not something people like to admit, especially in so serious a matter.

Lastly, Mother Nature may just have screwed it up. A big rainstorm on the body could eliminate every bit of evidence in one fell swoop.

It's good to keep in mind that sometimes there is evidence from a scene that has nothing to do with the killer. The evidence may be from a recent date or anyone who had previously been in the victim's house or car. Also, there may be evidence left by the paramedics or police officers called to the scene. Sometimes the scene is so poorly protected that there is evidence from everyone in town from the Mayor on down; everyone except the killer.

Handling the evidence is a lot trickier than people and juries imagine. More than one killer has been found not guilty in court because, in spite of overwhelming evidence against him, some tidbit of evidence from another person convinced the jury that someone else might have committed the crime.

DO SERIAL KILLERS EVER LEAVE THINGS AT THE CRIME SCENE TO CONFUSE THE POLICE?

Sometimes the killer might try to make the murder look like someone else did it. He might leave a misleading note, scribble some racist crap on the wall, or place a phony phone call to the police or family. He also might stage the body in

> "*Society right from the very beginning started to make me an animal...that's why I started all that killing.*"
>
> —ALBERT DE SALVO

143

such a way to make one think it is another kind of crime. This is fairly rare in a sexual homicide, and much more likely that a husband or boyfriend will stage a sexual homicide to cover up a domestic murder. Women who kill children may also try to make it look like an accident occurred to cover a smothering, beating, or strangulation.

Leaving erroneous DNA evidence is also a possibility. Bringing someone else's semen, clothes or hair is a pretty clever thing to do. Luckily, most serial killers don't think they will be caught anyway, so they don't usually work that hard at trying to confuse the jury.

DO SERIAL KILLERS EVER PLAY MIND GAMES WITH THE POLICE?

Just because Jack the Ripper, the Zodiac Killer, and David Berkowitz did it doesn't mean they all do! Initiating a cat-and-mouse game with the police is an extremely rare occurrence. The less contact with the police the serial killer has, the better off he is.

> *Satan gets into people and makes them do things they don't want to.*
>
> —HERBERT MULLIN

There are occasions when the killer will socialize with police at a known law enforcement hangout and try to get information on how the murder investigation is going, but he will rarely actively involve the police by playing games. Letters and other transmissions are now very easily traced, and even the bit of spit he used on the back of the stamp to send his nifty letter from six states away can hold evidence—something he cannot afford to do. Even if the killer is very careful with his communications, he may eventually become a victim of bad luck; or, if the police release copies of the communications, someone out there might eventually be able to identify him.

This is what befell one very unusual pair of serial killers, John Allen Muhammad and John Lee Malvo, who got big thrills out of playing with the police and the media. Muhammad, the leader of the pair, was willing to raise the stakes in his quest for power and control because he had reached a point in his life where only the most exciting and history-making crime would do. Muhammad enjoyed making the police jump through hoops and having his crimes broadcast nationally for all the country to watch. In the end, these communications led to his and Malvo's arrest. By a bizarre twist of fate, Muhammad's phone call to the police bragging about a previous homicide in another state led to the discovery of a fingerprint left at that scene that had never been properly run through all the databanks. This police error might never have been uncovered if the killers' desire to play games with the police had not gotten the better of them. This foolish behavior quickly ended the sniping "career" of John Allen Muhammad and John Lee Malvo.

The more likely scenario for the average serial killer to have the opportunity to play mind games occurs if the police actually show up to question the killer or bring him in for an interview. He may get some kind of kick out of convincing them what a great guy he is or misleading them. The killer knows, though, he should be careful that they don't get suspicious and start focusing on him. If that happens, then he can't operate as freely, and this might cut down on his fun.

DO SERIAL KILLERS EVER WANT TO GET CAUGHT?

> "More you do it, the better you like it."
> —*SUSAN ATKINS*

Sometimes a killer will turn himself in or confess. This is usually because the police are about to catch him anyway, and he thinks this is a better way to cut a deal.

Serial killers want to be free like anyone else and do what they like to do (kill) any time they please. They have committed their crimes with little to no remorse, so it's hard to believe that they would suddenly feel bad and give themselves up. We often read in some profiler's stories how clever interviewing techniques made them feel really bad and then they confessed. Although the techniques may be good, the confession is more likely to come from the feeling that they are trapped rather than feelings of guilt. Sometimes a killer trying to talk himself out of trouble talks himself into it instead and then loses the battle.

Going back to everyone's favorite serial killer, Ted Bundy, it has been asserted that at the end of his criminal career he "wanted to be caught" and that's why he was being so sloppy about what he was doing. When you think about it, this is actually a pretty lame statement. Bundy had been caught, and he was on the run. He knew it wasn't going to be long before he would be spending quality prison time; he was simply "filling his canteen before crossing the desert."

Then, once in a while, a killer breaks this rule. He actually does turn himself in for reasons no one can quite figure. Maybe he's getting bored and wants to get glory for his past crimes; maybe he thinks he can get more for turning himself in than by staying free. Because it's such a rare occurrence, and since serial killers are not usually known for telling the truth, it's hard to determine if the reason he gives is actually valid.

CAN A SERIAL KILLER PASS A POLYGRAPH?

It is thought that since a serial killer is such a practiced pathological liar he can easily fool a polygraph (SHE tech talk—lie detector test). However, there is a big difference between being a good liar and not knowing you are lying. A

> *"What I did was not for sexual pleasure. Rather it brought me some peace of mind."*
> —ANDREI CHIKATILO

polygraph depends on the body acting differently with lies than with truths.

Much of the problem with the results of polygraphs comes from the actual administration of the test. A good polygrapher is exceptionally important in turning out a test of any worth. Not only should a polygrapher be good at conducting the test itself, but he should also be a good interviewer, interrogator, and reader of body language.

The polygraph is really a tool for investigative purposes and not just a truth machine. This is why it is inadmissible in court. So much depends on the polygrapher and the circumstances that the results cannot be taken as absolute. However, if the test is well handled, quite a lot of information can be gleaned from it.

To administer the test properly, the subject should be notified in advance (at least a day or so) of the test. He should be well-rested and told not to take medicines that would change his reactions (some polygraphers start this process with a blood or urine test just to make sure). He should have his normal breakfast, and when he arrives, he should be well briefed on how the test will work and allowed to smoke if this is normal for him. He should not be intimidated in any way, shape or form.

It is often intimidation that invalidates so many police polygraphs; the subject takes the test under duress, and it is administered under stressful conditions. Often it is given by the police department itself, which makes the subject even more nervous. The polygraph questions must also be phrased properly and without any ambiguity: "Do you feel responsible for her death?" is a poor question. Perhaps the poor sod felt he should have given the woman a ride home from the bar and thereby prevented her death. He didn't kill her, but he now looks guilty because the question was not worded correctly. It would have been better to ask clearly, "Did you kill Susan?" If the subject fails the test or it comes back inconclusive, it is hard to know if it was the fault of the examiner or the suspect.

Properly done, if a suspect fails his test or appears deceptive on any of his answers, the polygrapher can then attempt to get closer to the truth with a specific line of questioning. The police can use those results to focus their investigation on a particular individual or some aspect of the test the individual failed.

There are times when a serial killer might pass a polygraph. Therefore, it is important to take all investigative information into account before deleting him from the suspect list.

HOW RELIABLE ARE WITNESSES AND TIPS IN SOLVING SERIAL HOMICIDES?

Countless investigations have been completely thrown off course because of completely erroneous information. A neighbor sees a truck in the neighborhood some time near the time of the homicide and reports its presence to the police. The public is asked for any information on this truck, and 300 people call in saying they saw that truck on that street. First of all, the truck may or may not even exist, it may have been some innocent person driving down the street, and how the heck do 300 people see that same truck in the period of a few minutes?

> *"I carried it too far, that's for sure."*
>
> —JEFFREY DAHMER

Meanwhile, hundreds of police man-hours are wasted.

It is far better to canvass the neighborhood with specific questions for the neighbors than to ask for any information someone might have. When an open question is presented to the public, thousands of people call with a whole lot of irrelevant information; and because so many calls come in, a tip line is set up with a whole bunch of unskilled people answering it. This means a real tip among the mass of useless information can get lost, misfiled, or never followed up on.

By asking specific questions like "Have you seen these shoes the killer left?" or "Does anyone know a person who ended up with a used Mickey Mouse watch in their possession without a particularly good reason for it?", the public knows what information is actually desired and the number of tips coming in will be more focused and useful.

Another problem is witnesses who seem to do very poorly with memory and description. Experiments have shown many people are quite a ways off in their descriptions of people, vehicles, or events. Some are so off the mark, it is hard to imagine where they even came up with the erroneous information. One must be careful with this information and analyze who gave the description as well as analyzing the description itself.

DO PSYCHICS REALLY HELP POLICE FIND BODIES OF VICTIMS AND HELP SOLVE SERIAL HOMICIDES?

You can fool most of the people most of the time.

> "A clown can get away with murder."
> —JOHN WAYNE GACY

For some reason, the myth of psychics helping police solve crimes lives on. Even though there are only a few unsubstantiated tales of psychics actually being right about anything, the police continue to use them and families still get bilked out of their money and allow their emotions to be manipulated.

I have seen the results of a number of psychics who have "helped" families with the cases I've worked on. The results of more than one psychic contacted about a particular case often have radically different "information." How can this be when only one set of events occurred during the crime? Of course the excuse is that one of the psychics may not be that good, or they are seeing different aspects of the crime.

Because serial killers are so rarely caught and these cases are not solved very often, the psychics can pretty much say whatever they want and no one can prove them wrong (kind of like a lot of profilers and their profiles!).

How do psychics actually come up with their stuff? Pretty much like any other con artist. They understand human nature. They will tell a family what they want to hear. They also use plain old logic. In the case of Alicia Showalter Reynolds, who went missing in Virginia in 1996, a number of psychics came forward to tell us all where her body was. In a field or in a barn were the top answers. Because the area she disappeared in used to be farm country, those were pretty good guesses. However, her body was found in a logging area. Oops! Guess no one realized that area was tucked in there. On occasion, a psychic gets lucky and guesses right. If you only advertise your wins and never your losses, it looks like you actually have some real ability.

Sometimes psychics go so far as to actually travel to an area and gather information before contacting the police or family. Then they claim to have never been there. The details of the "reading" are so specific (a large gnarled oak tree by a strange red building with no roof), that when those locations are found, it seems so uncanny that the psychic is then believed. Many body searches have been conducted on the word of psychics, and a whole lot of land gets dug up for nothing.

Why do police use psychics? Because they are usually free, make the family happy that the police are willing to try another tactic, and are not as threatening to the investigators as the other investigative or profiling experts who would be looking at the case information and notes. Over 70% of police departments have at some time used the services of a psychic.

Also, there are police investigators who buy into this stuff just like the rest of the public. Staged shows on television by psychics and a whole lot of phony publicity can make it seem like psychics really are psychic and worth taking the chance.

HOW MANY SERIAL HOMICIDES ARE ACTUALLY SOLVED?

> *When asked if he wore the skin face masks over a prolonged time:*
>
> *"Not too long, I had other things to do."*
>
> —ED GEIN

Not enough.

It is horrifying when you realize how few serial homicides cases are ever closed. A number of these cases are lost causes to begin with. When one adds to this number poor investigative techniques, lack of case linkage, evidence debacles, confused juries, all the cases no one even counts as serial homicides because they were never labeled as such, and all the cases that were closed erroneously (tacked on to dead guys or incarcerated felons even though there wasn't ample proof that those murders were committed by them), the percentage of solved cases is extraordinarily low.

Unfortunately, it is impossible to give statistics here. The actual data on these homicides is not available for analysis because it has never been realistically collected, and the rest of the information we are handed, as noted above, is questionable. In other words, I have no idea what the closure rate really is, but it doesn't look very good.

With or without an actual number, it is clear something needs to change in the methodology of investigating and prosecuting serial homicide cases.

THE PRACTICAL
PROFILE

What profiling is really about

HOW MUCH CAN YOU FIND OUT ABOUT THE KILLER FROM THE CRIME SCENE?

From 1940 to 1956 "The Mad Bomber" terrorized New York City. Police were overwhelmed with the cases that had gone on for so long unsolved. The crimes were reasonably simple and non-lethal, with the bombs usually being found before they exploded. The first bomb was discovered in a wooden toolbox, unexploded with a note that read "Con Edison crooks, this is for you." From there the crimes escalated with Consolidated Edison as the primary focus of their fury—some with notes, others without. It wasn't until December of 1956 that one of the bombs exploded and left six people injured.

> *" Society's had their chance. I'm going hunting. Hunting humans. "*
> —JAMES OLIVER HUBERTY

The public was whipped into a frenzy and demanded that the Mad Bomber be brought to justice. Police were overwhelmed, had little evidence other than the bombs themselves, and were uncertain as to the best course of action. The police finally decided to enlist the help of a Manhattan-based criminal psychiatrist, Dr. James A. Brussel. Brussel took the pile of evidence the police supplied and produced what is now known as the "first" official criminal profile.

Brussel concluded from the evidence that the bomber was likely male, middle-aged, meticulous, largely self-educated, Eastern-European and probably Catholic, living with female relatives and, more importantly, that he would have worked for Consolidated Edison or one of its subsidiaries. Dr. Brussel then went into detail as to what he thought would be the best way to capture the elusive bomber. The police would have to publicize the case and his profile widely. He also suggested they have Con Edison search its files of past employees. Brussel made a final damning statement about the bomber: "When you catch him, and I have no doubt you will, he'll be wearing a double-breasted suit. And it will be buttoned."

When the police finally arrested George Metesky for the bombings, the similarities to the profile were uncanny. Police arrived at Metesky's home, which he shared with his two sisters, to find him in his bathrobe. They allowed him to dress, and Metesky emerged from the apartment wearing a double-breasted suit, buttoned.

Ever since the media got hold of this profile and its eerie accuracy, the profiler has been seen as part master psychologist, part master intuitive.

Now let's logically pick apart the profile and see what all the noise is really about.

How in the world did Brussel narrow down the bomber to an ex-employee of Con Edison?

Wow, this is quite incredible! What behaviors in bomb-making tipped him off? Could it be the letters he attached to some of the bombs that raged at Con Edison's "dastardly deeds"? Obviously, Con Edison had pissed someone off, and this would most likely be an ex-employee. The fact that Brussel had to suggest this fact to the police makes one a little concerned about the quality of police investigators in that jurisdiction.

How did he come to all the personal conclusions about Metesky himself and his living situation?

Brussel's first conclusion that the bomber was a middle-aged man is a bit of a gimme. Bomb-making is not something most women are into, and as he had been at large for 16 years, it's not likely that his rage against Con Edison started as a toddler, but rather as a young adult. And now, 16 years later, he would be in his 40's.

Naturally he would be "largely self-educated" since they don't teach Bombing 101 at the local community college, and he had to learn this stuff somewhere. Continuing on from the conclusion that he worked at Con Edison, and that he was capable of constructing bombs, he was at least somewhat intellectual and careful in his work (bomb-making is not one of those things you want to mess up on in the lab). It was safe to assume that since he's still in a blue-collar job, his smarts didn't stem from a long college career.

Detailing his meticulousness was easy to conclude from the crimes. There were no prints left on any of the bombs, and he was careful about placing them, the majority of the time, in places where either they would be found before going off or would explode without a lot of casualties. He wasn't out to kill; he was trying to make a statement.

The letters attached to each of the bombs were written in near-perfect English using terms that were not common parlance for "Americans." It was concluded from this that he was an immigrant who had been part of the influx of Eastern Europeans in the 1930s and '40s, bringing with him his religious background, which would more than likely be Catholic.

New York is an expensive place to live; immigrant families often flush to the outskirts and stick together as a family. Living with any relative, female or not, would be expected.

What about the double-breasted suit?

This is the most logical conclusion of them all, actually. In that era, the double-breasted suit was a popular style with gentlemen. He has already been profiled as meticulous, so he's not likely to show up for police in flippers and a tutu, but well put together, clean and buttoned.

Are you saying that Dr. Brussel was a fake?

Not at all! Actually, Dr. Brussel did a fine job logically analyzing the evidence, and most of his conclusions were based on the facts. He did, in fact, exactly what a profiler should do.

Dr. Brussel's profile was glorified and held up as an incredible feat of criminology, not by illustrating how he came to his logical conclusions, but instead, by twisting things to make it seem like the good doctor had practically pulled his conclusions from thin air.

Unfortunately, many of today's ideologies about profiling stem from this distortion of Brussel's work. Many profiles contain conclusions that simply have no basis in any of the evidence of a crime. For example, to determine that a killer is twenty-five years of age, drives a truck, and has a knife collection because a woman is found raped and stabbed to death in a local park is pushing it.

However, we can draw logical conclusions about many characteristics of the killer from the crime scene and "victimology" (SHE definition—information about the victim that connects her to the killer and the crime).

For example, how can one determine what kind of car the killer drives? If he didn't use one in the actual crime, there is no way to determine this. The best one can do is guess based on what kind of character he is. Since serial killers are usually losers, the profiler tends to say, "He drives an older

159

vehicle…" There is no actual proof that this is true; he may have just come into some money, or his uncle may have died and passed a nice car down to him. While it is an interesting thought, this kind of information should not be included in the profile without some strong caveats that this is just a generalization for people included in the wide world of losers.

If, on the other hand, the killer did use a vehicle in the commission of his crime, we might be able to actually determine more about it by the actual evidence left behind. Tire prints and fibers obviously would give actual physical evidence of the type of vehicle. Size of the vehicle may be determined by the victim or victims put into it. If there are two killers and a couple of victims, the small sports car with no back seat isn't going to be the vehicle used. If there is evidence that the victim lay in a completely prone position for hours on the floor of a vehicle, then a car is not the likely vehicle in question, but rather a van or truck should be looked for.

Race is difficult to determine, and far too many profilers just toss out Caucasian because so many known serial killers have been white. Race is best determined by physical evidence left at the scene and specific elements of dumpsites and neighborhoods.

Determining the educational level of a killer is also a sticky subject. Movies and television have taught most criminals (even the dumb ones) that they should wipe down the crime scene to eliminate their prints. Since most killers rarely go to college, and high schools often graduate students who can't read, it is hard to guess any level of schooling for serial killers. Even if a woman is abducted off the university campus, this does not indicate the killer is from that campus and just because a woman with a master's degree is seen leaving the bar with some guy, doesn't mean that guy has an educational level equivalent to hers. Educational levels are best left out of profiles unless there is something specific to point to the killer's academic skills.

Profiling is a logical process where each aspect of the crime is analyzed carefully and placed into a dynamic psychological picture of the killer. Erroneous conclusions in a profile can bump an investigation off track, so everything presented in the profile must make sense to each aspect of the crime—psychologically and forensically.

How do you know if you are dealing with a serial killer?

A good adage would be "Unless proven otherwise, consider any homicide a possible serial killing." This is a good thing to keep in the back of one's mind when looking at any other homicide that comes along for possible connections. This is especially true in cases of sexual homicides. While other kinds of killings—rage, revenge, gang, financial gain murders—may only happen once in a lifetime, guys who decide to cross the line to rape and murder are exceptionally scary,

> *"After my head has been chopped off, will I still be able to hear, at least for a moment, the sound of my own blood gushing from my neck? That would be the pleasure to end all pleasures."*
>
> —PETER KURTEN

because they genuinely enjoy it. They enjoy it so much that it's very likely that they will do it again.

A sexual homicide should always be considered the work of a serial killer or potential serial killer. The investigator should always explore backwards in time (and be ready for the next murder), searching for other homicides this character could have committed. He should also search the histories of nearby jurisdictions and inform them of the homicide he is investigating.

Likewise, a profiler should be brought in (unless the police investigator is a profiler in his own right) to analyze the elements of any sexual homicide. It is not necessary to wait until someone decides there is a series of connected homicides that might benefit from profiling. Until recently, engaging the help of a profiler has been a last desperate attempt at solving a series of killings, and the profiler is only brought in after the public or the victim's family gets pretty bent out of shape at the fact no one has been caught. If a profiler is brought in at the beginning of the series, when there is just one sexual homicide to deal with, valuable information might be gained and the killer caught before there is a series to contend with and the serial killer gets better at what he does.

IF YOU HAVE A NUMBER OF CONNECTED CRIMES, CAN YOU TELL WHERE THE KILLER LIVES?

Determining where a suspect lives by where he commits his crimes is known as geographical profiling. It's a grand idea, except serial killers tend to move so much that by the time there are three crime locations, he might have moved a half dozen times. Add to this "minor" problem the possibility that the crimes aren't actually connected to

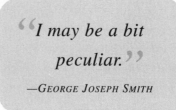

"I may be a bit peculiar."
—GEORGE JOSEPH SMITH

begin with, and plugging your variable into some computer program and coming up with a correct answer seems a bit improbable.

However, the concepts behind geographical profiling have some merit. Humans tend to find comfort in their own territories and in those that are similar. They tend to commit their crimes in locations they feel they have control over and are unlikely to just kill willy-nilly all over the place. We cannot ignore geography in any sexual homicide, but it is still a best bet to start in the neighborhood, fully understanding that our killer may have already packed up and moved.

Boundaries can represent not only physical obstacles, but also mental obstacles. Highways, rivers, the edge of the neighborhood: All can play a part in where a killer decides to commit crimes. The killer may be unwilling to cross over these boundaries. On the other hand, sometimes the killer purposefully chooses to cross those boundaries in order to confuse the investigators. He may choose to jump just across the county line so that two police departments will have to try to get along, or he may hope to make investigators think the killer lives in the next county over.

Geographical profiling is very useful in other crimes. Arsonists and burglars are easily found within close proximity of their crimes. However, arson fires and burglaries tend to happen in rapid succession without much of a break between incidents, indicating that the criminal is likely to be a local.

Because serial killers tends to take more time between each incident, there is a higher likelihood that the killer will either change residence or employment, increasing the odds that he'll kill in another area.

HOW DO YOU KNOW IF A PROFILE IS ANY GOOD?

It would seem the obvious answer is "You catch the guy and he matches!"

> "*I've got to get rid of the bodies, and you've got to help me.*"
> —CLAUDE DALLAS

However, this is not necessarily true. It is not the profile that catches serial killers; police investigators do. Profilers do not create a profile so good that all the detective needs to do is look up his address in the white pages and send a patrol car over to pick him up. The profile is only an investigative tool that helps police determine avenues of investigation to focus on. Good solid police work is what is necessary to bring the killer in.

Even if a profile ends up "matching" the killer, one has to look carefully at the reasons why. The more vague the profile, the more likely one is to be correct.

The best profile is not one that worries about "winning." A good profile gives complete explanations for any determination made, allowing the investigators to analyze for themselves how useful this information is. The more evidence one has to work with, the more accurate a profile is likely to be. Bad profile information can completely throw an investigation off the mark, so it is best that the profiler work with the investigators, asking questions, going to the scene if possible, and seeking out more information on his own. A good profile is also dynamic and can be changed as new evidence comes in. It is clear and well-thought-out, so it is a teaching tool for investigators to learn from and assist them in future investigations as well.

WHAT IS THE DIFFERENCE BETWEEN A DETECTIVE AND A PROFILER?

> "I have no particular desire to live. I have no particular desire to be killed. It is a matter of indifference to me. I do not think I am altogether right."
>
> —ALBERT FISH

There are detectives who are excellent profilers and profilers who are excellent detectives. Either of these combinations would be extraordinarily beneficial to any investigation.

Profiling is a combination of understanding the criminal mind, understanding forensics, understanding victims, understanding the investigation, and having the logic to put together pieces of the puzzle. Some detectives have all of these skills themselves and have increased these skills through study and practice. However, many detectives really don't have a lot of training in some of these areas, which leaves a bit of a hole when it comes to analyzing certain crimes like sexual homicides.

There are some police investigators who readily admit that their experience with sexual homicides is limited, as these crimes are not as common in their jurisdictions as other felonies. This is when a profiler can bring his or her ability to the police investigation. Especially in the smaller department where personnel is limited and sexual homicides are few, the profiler can be a temporary member of the investigative team. During that time period, the profiler can help not only with that particular crime but also train the detectives to do some of the future profiling themselves.

A frustrated investigator who has been working on a particular sexual homicide for a long time may feel he has exhausted all the options in his investigation. Calling in an outside profiler is a way to get a fresh look at evidence from someone who has no ties to the city and may be able to see things from a different and helpful point of view.

Profilers deal with case after case of sexual homicide which tends to hone their skills specific to these crimes. It's like seeing a doctor when you have chest pains: your regular internist will be able to help you, but it's usually a pretty good idea to get the opinion of a cardiologist as well.

THROW AWAY THE KEY!

Prison and rehabilitation

DO SERIAL KILLERS EVER FEEL BAD ABOUT THE CRIMES THEY HAVE COMMITTED?

Well, they feel really bad about being caught. Does that count?

> **"*I'm sorry I killed five people, okay?*"**
>
> —GARY ALAN WALKER

It's always amazing to watch the remorse start to flow from a serial killer after he's spent a decade or two in prison and it's time for the parole hearing or the execution chamber. They suddenly find "God" or "Jesus" or "Allah" when they realize that they, themselves, are somehow going to be inconvenienced. One has to wonder where all the remorse was while they listened to the screams of their victims begging them for mercy.

The sorrow they feel isn't for the family of his victims; it's not even for his victims directly. The psychopathic nature of the serial killer prohibits him from really caring about anyone beyond himself. The sorrow he feels is for himself, his lack of freedom, and the end of his life.

During their time in prison, serial killers rarely break down even so far as to admit that they alone were responsible for their acts. They usually elaborate on some dreadful childhood happening that made them a killer. More often, there is an absolute refusal on the part of these men to admit they acted on their own account and the choices they made to kill were to satisfy their own selfish needs. It's always somebody else's fault, they are not really guilty, they were just acting out against the abuse they suffered at some point.

Some killers issue apologies as their final words to the families they have destroyed; yet even these apologies don't offer much in the way of remorse for their acts directly. It's "I'm sorry you lost your daughter;" never "I'm sorry that I found it really fun to listen to your daughter screaming in pain, and that the last emotion she felt was fear of me."

Am I being too harsh here? Hmmm… then ask yourself this acid question: if the serial killer were not incarcerated, would he feel this sorrow; or would he still be out there killing?

WHY DO SERIAL KILLERS WRITE BOOKS ABOUT THEIR CRIMES?

Bragging rights, fame, and a little misplaced respect, usually.

When the serial killer is out killing, he's the master of his world. But he's terribly lonely, isolated as he has always been from society. He's socially retarded, unable to maintain a relationship, and just downright creepy. Once he's arrested, charged, and convicted, he becomes a celebrity.

Finally in a position where what he says is gripping, he can brag about his kills and let journalists and groupies peer into his evil serial killer mind. Here is a guy who has never had a successful relationship in his life, has been a failure at everything he's ever tried to do, and just for killing a few women he's now seen as a monster and one of the greatest criminal minds in history. What a deal!

> "*I wished I could stop but I could not. I had no other thrill or happiness.*"
> —DENNIS NILSEN

Then, from the depths of the mind of the greatest serial criminal in history, comes the need to write. In a book he can talk about his master plans, his many kills, and how easy it was for him to dodge the police. He lands TV interviews and has women falling in love with him—far more attention than he ever would have had as the weird guy who lived in the stinky trailer.

By manipulating the system, he gets what he's wanted from the beginning: Power.

IF A SERIAL KILLER GIVES DETAILS OF HIS CRIME, CAN WE BELIEVE HIM?

> "*Sometimes I feel like a vampire.*"
> —TED BUNDY

To some extent, yes, you can. But you must remember that this will be *his* version of events that he's played over in his head thousands of times. It will eventually blend in neatly with the fantasy he created before, and it will be hard to distinguish between what he's actually done and what he's been fantasizing for so many years.

In Stanley Kubrick's film *A Clockwork Orange*, we get to know Alex DeLarge, a young psychopath who takes us through an autobiographical journey of his crimes, incarceration, and "rehabilitation." Many critics trashed the film for its over-choreographed violent scenes, saying they were glorified, inaccurate, and not *really* how violent acts play out. What these critics failed to note was that the story was being told from Alex's point of view, and that it was how *he* remembered it. It was all-perfect in its progression, and he always emerged the victor.

This is how the "autobiographical" accounts of serial killers must be taken. You must remember that the lines between fantasy and reality no longer exist in his mind, and he's simply telling his version of what transpired, hoping to milk the fact that since he's the only person at the crime who is still alive, his word will be taken as it stands, regardless of embellishment.

He can be trusted to give some details of the crime quite honestly. This is his chance to show off his only accomplishment in life. But what he says must always be taken with a grain of salt. When giving a full account, the nature of the psychopath is to twist things to make him look better. To illustrate he's an innocent victim of society, he'll preface his tales with stories of childhood abuse. To horrify and make you fear him, he will embellish on the atrocity of his crimes; and an outright plea of innocence will more than likely be laden with conspiracy theories and things that "just happened."

HOW DO SERIAL KILLERS GET ON IN PRISON?

Most of them do pretty well, actually. Often earning status as a "trustee" and working nicely into the strict regimen of prison, the serial killer really has no choice but to "do well"—those who don't end up in solitary cells.

When a person is told when to eat, sleep, and move, and is monitored all day, every day, to make certain that he

> *"We all go a little mad sometimes."*
> —NORMAN BATES

conforms to the rules, it makes it easy for that person to toe the line and seem like a very nice, rehabilitated boy.

If you take an alcoholic and put him in a setting where he has no access to alcohol whatsoever, in time he can brag about how sober he is and how he can control his urges to drink to the point where he no longer needs to. The true test of his sobriety comes when he's out of the controlled situation and faced with an open bar.

The deal is the same with the serial killer. When he's removed from his victims of choice, not allowed contact or the resources to feed his desires, and essentially placed in a vacuum, naturally he's going to behave. But what happens when he leaves that vacuum and is faced with an opportunity to kill? Are we willing to take the chance with *our own* children to test his rehabilitation?

The psychopathology of the serial killer started in the earliest years of his life; from the time he's a small child he's learning and developing his predatory behaviors. A combination of what he's learned and the personality he was born with determines who he is and what he feels he needs to do to fulfill his needs. In prison, he's not allowed to act on his needs. Feeling confined at first, the killer quickly learns other ways to vent his needs for power and control. And in prison the best way to gain that is to be an extra good boy and earn extra privileges.

CAN A SERIAL KILLER JUST STOP KILLING?

You bet. Contrary to the notion that a serial killer will keep killing until he is physically unable to because of health, age or imprisonment, serial killers can just stop. And some do.

Like the pornography he started out with, sometimes even killing gets boring, or seems too risky to do anymore since the police (or his wife) look like they might be catching on. He can go back to being a voyeur, or "merely" rape and set his urges to kill aside.

> *" I have no desire whatever to reform myself. My only desire is to reform people who try to reform me, and I believe the only way to reform people is to kill 'em. "*
>
> —CARL PANZRAM

Some predators progress steadily on to rape, and when the first kill happens, they don't actually enjoy it and revert back to raping. There is a lot of work involved in being a serial killer: hiding bodies, cleaning up evidence, working out alibis; and some rapists are happy enough with the humiliation and fear they can cause by rape. For some, there's the added thrill of leaving the victim alive, since you know that someone on the planet will always be afraid of you and remember exactly what you did.

HOW CAN SOME WOMEN FALL IN LOVE WITH AND MARRY SERIAL KILLERS IN PRISON?

Sometimes, ya' just wish the answers to these questions were easy. There seem to be three distinct groups of women who fall in love with serial killers.

> "*Me? I wouldn't hurt no broads. I love broads.*"
>
> —ALBERT DE SALVO

The first group is the extra-kind-hearted (dumb?) "I can change him" type who believes that serial killers are just misunderstood and vulnerable men who suffered terrible abuse, and with the love of the right woman can become "normal." This is also the kind of woman who will stay with a man who beats her regularly, hoping she can "save him from himself." At least for this particular type, she is safer than the battered woman she most likely would be, because "her lover" will probably spend their entire marriage behind bars where he can't knock her around. (However, being behind bars doesn't prevent emotional and financial abuse).

Then there are the real "groupies"—fans of serial killers who find their exploits morbidly fascinating. They're not particularly interested in changing these guys; they actually find the naughty serial killer thing sexy and mysterious. Like musician groupies, they flock to these untouchable men hoping for any sort of attention. It's the forbidden bad-boy thing, and when the killer returns her letter telling her how lonely he is in prison and how he just wants the company of a woman, she thinks she is something special. She's likely to ask questions about his crimes and gullibly take in the crap he feeds her about all that he's done. She happily thrives on the idea of being the "lover" of a serial killer; it brings her attention like she's never had before. Sure, Christy is dating a biker, but I'm the lover of a vicious serial killer.

The final, and scariest, group is thankfully very rare. These women are psychopaths themselves and seem to thrive on living vicariously through their lovers. They have some elements of the "groupie" as they enjoy the shock factor of "loving" a serial killer. But this last type loves sharing the "dirty little secrets" with her lover and asks him to tell of his deeds over and over.

This is also the kind of woman who happily cranks out graphic books, "exploits" the serial killer, and creates fame for herself. In her book, she'll detail his crimes in brutal detail. Then, in the bright light of the media, she becomes the loving wife/girlfriend/confidante and will discuss how she managed to see past his evil side and how the journey to the execution chamber has changed her forever. But now that he's dead, she's moved on to yet another death-row inmate and she can now write detailed accounts of *his* crimes….

THE PROFILER

A look into the personal life of a profiler

ARE PROFILERS AFRAID THAT SERIAL KILLERS WILL COME AFTER THEM?

This is another really good invention of Hollywood and profilers who want folks to think they are some kind of profiling *Shaft*! Serial killers are wimps, which is why they pick easy victims to begin with. They're sure as heck not going to go after some person with police connections and a shotgun.

> " *These children that come at you with knives, they are your children. You taught them. I didn't teach them. I just tried to help them stand up.* "
>
> —CHARLES MANSON

Most profilers are not even actively involved in any investigating work. They sit in their libraries or in the police station mulling over the evidence and photographs, writing reports, and making suggestions. On occasion, they go to prisons to do interviews. They are not pissing off anyone in particular.

Investigative Criminal Profilers (SHE definition—criminal profilers who also actually go into the field and investigate) run a higher risk of physical danger. Traveling to the communities where the homicides have occurred, the investigative criminal profiler may go to the crime scenes and retrace the steps of the victim and killer, reinterview witnesses and suspects within the town, go to the press to stir things up, and run down new leads. Sometimes the profiler can end up in some not-so-great neighborhoods talking to people who are not exactly sterling citizens. Also, it may turn out that the homicide was not actually committed by a serial killer, but some other kind of more volatile criminal. It may happen that the person who is supposed to be *only* a witness turns out to be the killer, and the profiler finds himself with him inside the killer's home. These are far stickier situations, and the investigative criminal profiler must take measures to be sure he doesn't end up another unsolved homicide.

DO PROFILERS HAVE A CRIMINAL MIND?

Heavens no! Profilers never have a wicked thought, are extraordinarily moral and ethical, have never even committed the mildest of crimes (like inhaling), and only have one defect.

> **"The more I looked at people, the more I hate them."**
> —CHARLIE STARKWEATHER

We are pathological liars.

Seriously (and I hope you didn't actually take me seriously), any profiler worth his salt has at least a very strong understanding of how criminals think, which no doubt was gained by hanging around them in some way, shape, or form. Either he has worked with criminals for a long time, or has been so unlucky as to have a whole crew of criminals clinging to the family tree.

Understanding criminal behavior is important to profiling. But you also have to have a deep understanding of human emotions in general and comprehend how different situations can cause people to act and react. For this reason, it is difficult for college students and young adults to totally comprehend the behaviors of killers and victims. Thankfully, they usually just don't have the life experience to make them this aware of the human condition. They find the crimes horrifically shocking (good!), and even if they're not shocked, they tend to romanticize the crime, applying psychobabble instead of logic. This is one job where the experience that comes with age is truly an advantage.

Students and young adults usually wrap themselves up in the biographical accounts of killers, carefully studying their actions and trying to pull some deeper meaning from them. What they tend to forget to do is conduct equally careful research into the life of the victim. There were at least two people at the crime scene, and the relationship and actions that transpired there are based on both their personalities.

Studying the killer without studying the victim is like reading every other page of a book.

Some profilers have spent all their time in classrooms and in books. While there is nothing wrong with good studies, if they haven't left this arena and mucked about in the real world, they are limiting their skills to theory. Going back to your chest pain and a trip to the cardiologist, it is a better idea to see the cardiologist who has at least seen, touched and worked with a human being with chest pain in person; not just read about them in books.

By having an understanding of both criminals and victims, a profiler can view the crimes as they do, understanding their choices and attitudes from both sides. This helps with linking crimes, investigative strategies, and interviewing. Then the profilers can help separate good suspects from the just weird folks and get these serial killers off the street and behind bars where they belong.

DO PROFILERS GET SO INTO THE MIND OF THE SERIAL KILLER THAT THEY FALL INTO "THE ABYSS" AND HAVE A HARD TIME COPING?

More than one profiler has written about this abyss and the horrible struggle not to allow the world of the serial killer to destroy their sanity. I have a piece of advice for these folks:

"GET OUT OF THE BUSINESS!" (You wuss!)

Any profiler who actually finds the serial killer's mentality merging with their own has serious issues they need to address. Some of us would have fired "Clarice" on her first day of work because she had an issue with bleating lambs. She needs help.

> *Whoever fights monsters should see to it that in the process he does not become a monster. And when you look into the abyss, the abyss also looks into you.*
>
> —FRIEDRICK NIETZSCHE

This is not to say that a profiler can't suffer from a high level of post-traumatic stress disorder (PTSD) (SHE definition—having problems coping in everyday life because of being involved in some horrifying or depressing circumstance like rape or war). Sometimes police officers, emergency medical personal and others who deal constantly with death, slimy people and the less-than-pleasant parts of life begin to get a very cynical and depressing attitude. As a cop once said to me, "You go to the circus with your kids and instead of seeing your fellow attendees as nice folks who brought their children out for a day of fun, you see them all as child molesters and drug dealers." Profilers may have similar issues as they go off for a lovely picnic with their families and survey their picnic ground as a really nice body dump site.

Many cops, emergency medical personnel, and profilers deal with death and violence constantly. Unlike a person in a "normal" profession who experiences death from a bit of a distance every year or five years and the rest of the time plants flowers and does needlepoint, these special groups of people get up in the morning to spend most of their waking moments dealing with violence and death. This can eventually take its toll on mental health.

Even plain ol' job stress causes people to work far too many hours, drink too much alcohol, and end up divorced and in poor health. For some workers, good emotional support, psychological counseling or perhaps a change of career becomes absolutely necessary.

However, even these folks aren't falling into any abyss and melding with any killer's mind. That kind of bizarre psychology is a sign of some serious problem or a desire to make one's book sell a million copies.

DO PROFILERS HAVE NIGHTMARES?

Many think because of the horrific images we see on a daily basis, our dreams will be peppered with dismembered bodies and serial killers stabbing us. Profilers have a pretty good mechanism for professional detachment with all the gruesome photos we must review. We have been known to fall asleep surrounded by eight-by-ten glossies of a crime scene in our beds, waking up at three in the morning to check out that gash in the neck and going back to sleep to dream about happy furry bunnies.

> *" The Demons wanted girls; sugar and spice and everything nice."*
> —DAVID BERKOWITZ

It is not that we are coldhearted. Looking at pictures of the victims when they were smiling and alive with their whole lives ahead of them is a heartbreaking experience, but in order to examine a crime scene effectively, you have to pull back and be objective. To cloud what you see with personal emotion is a terrible disservice to the people you are trying to help.

In all honesty, the toughest part of the job is dealing with the grief of the families. It's easy enough to turn off emotional attachment and spend hours analyzing forensic details to draw your conclusions as to what you believe transpired and why. "Why?" is the toughest question posed to the profiler, because you can't really provide answers that make a whole lot of moral sense. "Well, he thought it was fun," is not an answer that families want to hear; they'd rather hear about some psychotic episode and how their child was in the wrong place at the wrong time.

DO PROFILERS HAVE WEIRD LIVES?

I have to admit that profilers work in such a peculiar field that people think we are pretty weird. Like cops, emergency medical technicians, and coroners, our conversations lean toward the macabre; this tends to make people think we're kind of strange. Our constant contact with death and criminals freaks some people out, and while they enjoy being scared at a movie or reading true crime books, a lot of people really don't like the real world encroaching on their nice lives.

Profilers may find themselves with a select group of friends. They may also have to learn to talk about art and movies at cocktail parties and, unlike teachers and real estate agents, they may avoid discussions about work.

Children of profilers certainly see an interesting side of life: bookshelves filled with death investigation books and homicide textbooks, and the locked and forbidden crime photos drawer. Conversations about serial killers at the dinner table and having a parent who peruses more pornography sites than the local pervert make for an interesting childhood. Injuries and cuts may cause the parent profiler to be quite fascinated with the blood spatter pattern on the floor. On occasion, an older teenage child can be helpful in reconstructing crime scenes, and more than one child of a profiler has been "stabbed a few times" to check angles of assault while eating an ice cream cone and watching television. But then again, if the profiler were a tailor, his children would know the intricacies of a sewing machine and be pulled in to model something "for just a minute." It's work. Our children know what we do and they adapt.

Other than this, life goes on as normal.

HOW DO PROFILERS STAY SANE?

A black sense of humor and lots of wonderful, uplifting activities to keep us realizing that not all of life is a horrible joke.

> "*I can't take this anymore, them constantly insinuating I'm crazy.*"
>
> —*BETTY BRODERICK*

My rather dark sense of humor is probably evident in this book! It is somewhat the sick sense of humor as is used by others in similar professions. Jokes about death, bodies, and bad luck keep us from being totally grim every time we encounter such horrors. This in no way means we don't care; we just find something to lighten our mood.

Outside of perverse jokes, we enrich our lives with good, wholesome activities. Theatre, art, scuba diving, and travel—all of these things keep us balanced and able to get through the week.

DO PROFILERS HAVE SOME KIND OF PSYCHIC ABILITY THAT HELPS THEM ENVISION THE KILLER AND THE CRIME?

> *"I have no remorse. As to whether recollection of my deeds makes me feel ashamed, I will tell you. Thinking back to all the details is not at all unpleasant. I rather enjoy it."*
>
> —PETER KURTEN

No, we actually do profiling the hard way. We sweat over the answers.

If we were psychics, we would hardly need to bother with profiling skills. We could just charge a whole lot of money to come up with really useless answers like "The killer's name starts with an R and he lives in a blue house with at least two numbers that are three and seven."

We could even channel straight from the dead victim herself, and she could tell us that the killer's name starts with an R and he lives in a blue house with at least two numbers that are three and seven.

We wish we were at least telekinetic; then we wouldn't have to get up all the time looking for barf bags every time someone asks, "Are you psychic?"

Can you learn profiling, or is it a gift?

There has been an argument going on for ages in the pro-filing world about profiling. Is it an art or is it science, or is it both? Many aspects of profiling can be learned

> **"I gave up love and happiness a long time ago."**
> —Richard Ramirez

through education or experience, but there is still an innate ability to understand humans and solve puzzles that proba-bly can't be learned by just anyone.

Just as some have an ear for music and others a brain for math, profilers have to come hardwired with a basic ability and fascination with the subject in order for education and experience to build them into excellent profilers.

Can women profile and get into the mind of the male serial killer?

Absolutely! Many people are very skeptical that a female could understand the male desire to rape and murder, but if one understands basic human nature and the need for power and control, then these crimes are but a variation of this. The woman profiler can't be the kind of female who wants to understand the poor boy and make him all better. She has to

> "*I did this not as a sex act...but out of hate for her. I don't mean out of hate for her in particular, really I mean out of hate for a woman.*"
>
> —ALBERT DE SALVO

be the kind that can accept that some human beings are just plain ol' pieces of crap.

Oddly enough, sometimes men have difficulty profiling because they can't accept that another man could think that way! They shudder and say, "Well, that's just sick!" and just can't stand dealing with the guy at all.

DO PROFILERS EVER KNOW ANY SERIAL KILLERS PERSONALLY?

Some profilers have been in the same room with serial killers for interviews in prison, and some have met with them when they are still free and on the loose.

But we're not about to let them marry into the family or invite them over to the house for a family barbeque. We want them as far away from us as possible, preferably with a steel fence in between.

Pulling a serial homicide suspect in for an interview then bumping into them later at the supermarket makes for an interesting encounter. He'll stop and stare with a rather nasty look of defiance. Thanks to the media, profilers have been granted an interesting level of mystique, not too unlike that of the serial killer. Because of this, the serial killer has some preconceived notions of his own. Here he stands, making eye contact with someone he fears may be the only person in the world who knows exactly what he is and what he has done. To him, he is looking at his nemesis and the archenemy of his demented world; with fear and arrogance mixed together, he sends the message, "I am still out here. You can't beat me."

> "*I'm a mistake of nature.*"
>
> —ANDREI CHIKATILO

LAST QUESTION!

'Nuff said

How can I help stop serial killers?

Pay attention to sexual homicides in your area and give any assistance you can to law enforcement. Don't ignore those gut feelings that some weirdo's behavior is connected to a crime. Go to the authorities.

Support your local law enforcement with enough tax money to do their jobs. Under-funded police mean crimes don't get solved.

If the police aren't doing a good job handling a sexual homicide in your community, make a whole lot of noise.

> *"I was born with the devil in me. I could not help the fact that I was a murderer, no more than the poet can help the inspiration to sing."*
> —H.H. HOLMES

When your neighbors get raped and murdered, you should never let the police rest until justice is served. Don't just forget about the crime a week later and assume it's being investigated and by doing so ignore reality. Support the family of the victim by helping them see that the crime is solved and by rallying the community behind them. Make it clear to government officials and law enforcement that the citizens expect truth, justice, and public safety.

If you are a police officer, learn all you can about sexual predators and serial killers. Accept the help of profilers who specialize in this work, and use all the expert help you can get to solve a crime. Remember, this is not your case. It is the community's homicide case and the family's homicide case. You are just the public servant assigned to help. Also, learn more about victims and how to deal with the families of victims. They deserve the best treatment law enforcement can serve up for as many days, weeks, and years it takes to solve the homicide. Don't ever lie to them, and always call them back.

If you are a student, keep studying! Volunteer and take jobs working in any field related to criminals, victims, investigations or profiling. Read all the books you can and attend as many classes as you can.

And, finally, everyone can help stop serial killers by contributing to the totally pro bono work of The Sexual Homicide Exchange (SHE) at www.SHEprofilers.com.

GLOSSARY

Blitz Attack—A sudden, violent attack.

"Bop and Drop"—Any fast, violent maneuver that renders the victim unconscious or unable to fight.

"Crap Crimes"—Crimes that make you wonder why a person would bother to commit them.

"Criminals in Overdrive"—Criminals who have lost all regard for others and are on a spree consisting of several different types of crimes.

"Dead Woman in Field"—A generic term for a rural body discovery.

Frotteurism—The intentional (and unwelcome) rubbing or touching of a person or item that causes arousal; i.e., those guys who just happen to "rub up" against people as they walk by.

"Gone to Seed"—People who have lost their youthful physique due to age, childbearing, or Twinkies.

Grandiosity—Exaggerated self-worth.

Investigative Criminal Profiler—Profilers who go into the field to investigate a crime.

Linkage Blindness—Failing to see that separate crimes may be related or have been committed by the same person.

"Liquid Courage"—Any chemical a person takes in order to calm their nerves to commit a crime.

Locard's Exchange Principle—The theory that a person cannot enter a scene without leaving a bit of themselves behind, and taking a bit of the scene with them.

Modus Operandi (MO)—The basic things one needs to do to commit a crime.

Munchausen's Syndrome by Proxy (MSP)—A serious psychological condition in which an individual makes another person sick for some sort of gain, usually emotional. Children are most frequently the victims of this abuse.

Narcissism—"Me. Me. Me." When a person is so consumed with himself, his own pleasures and needs, that he fails to identify the needs of another.

"Natural Progression"—How a criminal evolves from petty to serious crimes.

One-off Crimes—One-time killings by a mad boyfriend or dealer in a drug deal gone bad.

Polygraph—A lie-detector test.

Post-offense Behavior—How a predator behaves after (s)he's committed a crime.

Post-Traumatic Stress Disorder (PTSD)—A condition that causes a person to have problems coping in everyday life because of being involved in some horrifying or depressing circumstance like rape or war.

Psychopath—A personality best described as "egocentric" and "anti-social"; includes excessive lying, delusions of grandeur, and superficial charm.

Psychotic—Behavior that convinces us that the individual had *no* clue to what was right or wrong, normal or abnormal, or if what he is doing at that moment is totally nuts.

RFLP, PCR, STR, & mtDNA Testing—Different DNA tests that require different amounts of specimen to run the test: RFLP—a lake, PCR—a puddle, STR—a drop, mtDNA—half a drop.

Sadism—When making another person suffer brings you pleasure.

Sexual Sadist—A person who becomes sexually aroused by purposefully inflicting pain or humiliation through perverse and painful sexual acts.

"Sneak and Stand"—Those guys who just "show up" behind you, seemingly out of nowhere.

Stalker—An individual obsessed with controlling another person, albeit initially through "friendly" means.

Validation—Input from another that reassures you of your behavior or actions, "He does it too, so I must not be a complete freak of nature!"

Victimology—Information that relates to the victim and their role in the crime.